Muslims

The religion of Islam is of vital concern to everyone in the contemporary world. Understanding what Muslims think about the modern world and how they react to its challenges is an important task for all who wish to locate Islam in contemporary life. Andrew Rippin focuses on how Muslims perceive the contemporary period and explores how they understand the Qur'an and the figure of Muhammad as relevant to life today.

Professor Rippin explains how, in Muslim contemporary life, a revealed, inherited world view is in tension with and changing alongside an emerging, newly discovered world view. He explores how these two world views are to be reconciled and analyses the various recommendations of selected Muslim thinkers. He looks at modern Muslim views on religious authority, including feminism's 'new Islam', and shows how these views affect the way Islam is enacted in individual lives.

Essential reading for all students and teachers of Islam and comparative religion, *Muslims: Volume 2* will also be of interest to readers concerned with understanding Islam as a religious force in the world and in the lives of individuals.

Andrew Rippin is Professor of Religious Studies at the University of Calgary, Canada. He is the author of *Muslims: Their Religious Beliefs and Practices. Volume 1: The Formative Period* (1990).

The Library of Religious Beliefs and Practices
Edited by John Hinnells
University of Manchester
and Ninian Smart
University of California at Santa Barbara

This series provides pioneering and scholarly introductions to different religions in a readable form. It is concerned with the beliefs and practices of religions in their social, cultural and historical setting. Authors come from a variety of backgrounds and approach the study of religious beliefs and practices from their different points of view. Some focus mainly on questions of history, teachings, customs and ritual practices. Others consider, within the context of a specific region or geographical region, the inter-relationships between religions; the interaction of religion and the arts; religion and social organization; the involvement of religion in political affairs; and, for ancient cultures, the interpretation of archaeological evidence. In this way the series brings out the multi-disciplinary nature of the study of religion. It is intended for students of religion, ideas, social sciences and history, and for the interested lay person.

Already published:

Zoroastrians
Their Religious Beliefs and Practices
Mary Boyce

Theravāda Buddhism
A Social History from Ancient Benares to Modern Colombo
Richard Gombrich

The British
Their Religious Beliefs and Practices
Terence Thomas

The Jains
Paul Dundas

Mahāyāna Buddhism
Paul Williams

Religions of South Africa
David Chidester

Muslims
Their Religious Beliefs and Practices. Volume 1: The Formative Period
Andrew Rippin

Muslims

Their religious beliefs and practices
Volume 2: the contemporary period

Andrew Rippin

London and New York

First published 1993
by Routledge
11 New Fetter Lane, London EC4P 4EE

Simultaneously published in the USA and Canada
by Routledge
29 West 35th Street, New York, NY 10001

© 1993 Andrew Rippin

Typeset in 10 on 12 pt Times by
NWL Editorial Services, Langport, Somerset

Printed and bound in Great Britain by
T.J. Press (Padstow) Ltd, Padstow, Cornwall

British Library Cataloguing in Publication Data
A catalogue record for this book is available from the British
Library

Library of Congress Cataloging in Publication Data
Rippin, Andrew, 1950–
    Muslims.
    (The Library of religious beliefs and practices)
    Includes bibliographical references and indexes.
    Contents: v. 1. The formative period – v. 2. The contemporary
    period.
    1. Islam. I. Title. II. Series.
BP161.2.R53   1990   297   89–10442
ISBN 0–415–04518–5 (v. 1)
ISBN 0–415–04519–3 (pbk.: v. 1)
ISBN 0–415–04527–4 (v. 2)
ISBN 0–415–04528–2 (pbk.: v. 2)

For my mother,
Margaret Rippin,
with love

Contents

Preface

In reviewing Volume 1 of this book, which deals with the formative period of Islam, some readers were led to wonder just what might be in store for Volume 2. In one sense, they were perfectly right to wonder. Volume 1 covers a very limited amount of material and there are vast expanses of Islamic intellectual thought which are in need of attention. The fact that this volume isolates the chronologically contemporary period should not be taken to suggest that the rest of Islamic history is of no importance or somehow uninteresting. By no means is this the case. The contents of the present volume reflect, rather, my perception of both current teaching tendencies in undergraduate university situations and the reading public's interest in Islamic matters. The contemporary period is one of vital concern and finding ways of explaining it to students and other interested parties is something that occupies much of my time and the time of many other university teachers like me.

On the other hand, the contents of Volume 2 of this work should really come as no surprise. Volume 1 deals with the three central components which came together to form classical Islam: the image of pre-Islamic times, Muhammad – the prophet of Islam, and the Qur'an – the scripture of Islam. The interaction of those elements provides the basis for a look at Muslim theology and law, as well as alternative visions of Islam. Given that basic understanding of the core of Islam, the coverage of this volume is quite predictable. The central issues to be raised relate to how Muslims perceive the contemporary period, and how they understand the Qur'an and the figure of Muhammad as interacting with, and being relevant to, the situation of the nineteenth and twentieth centuries. How these understandings (and they are emphatically multiple) have interacted to produce certain ramifications in Muslim contemporary life and thought becomes the task of the rest of the work. In sum, we are dealing with a revealed, inherited world view in tension with and changing alongside an emerging, newly discovered world view.

How these two world views are to be conceived and reconciled (if, indeed, that is the choice) is the issue to be faced in this book, along with the various recommendations which flow from that encounter in the opinion of selected Muslim thinkers.

Writing a work on modern Islam has never been an easy task and the current turmoil in various parts of the world – many of them Muslim – has certainly not made it any easier. The attempt to come to terms with what is going on in a very fluid situation has often made me long for the relative stability of the study of past history while writing this book. Even there, however, the value placed upon the past by various contemporary religious positions renders the security of writing about the anonymity of history illusory. To understand the reasons why the contemporary religious sensibility sees itself as having something at stake in the study of history, then, brings Volumes 1 and 2 of this book together in yet another way. The reflection upon manifestations of Islam in the past may be complemented by reflections upon the present.

Acknowledgements

A number of people have helped me with the writing of this book and I would like to extend my sincere thanks to them. My students Dan Fredrick, Nusrat Mirza, Christopher Buck and Floyd MacKay made significant contributions towards the accuracy and clarity of the text. Norman Calder and my editor, John Hinnells, were both extremely helpful in directing me towards a more coherent result. Todd Lawson aided me in many more ways than he imagines and, while the final product is certainly not the book he would have written, its present shape and form owes much to him. My partner Marion's love and encouragement benefited me in ways untold too many times.

Transliteration and other technical considerations

Considerations of printing costs have not allowed diacritical marks to be included in the Arabic words and names cited in this book. For a precise rendering of a given Arabic word and further information on any given topic, the reader should refer in the first instance to the *Encyclopaedia of Islam* (Leiden, E.J. Brill, first edition 1913–36, reprinted 1987; new edition in progress, 1960–, up to the letter 'n' so far; *Shorter Encyclopaedia of Islam*, 1953, gathers together articles on religion from the old edition with some updated material). This essential reference tool is arranged according to the Arabic terms and this often seems a hindrance for readers not well acquainted with the subject. An attempt has been made in this book, therefore, to include the relevant Arabic words in order to facilitate further reference through the *Encyclopaedia of Islam*. A problem arises, however, which makes this task more difficult than it should be. The transliteration system used in the *Encyclopaedia of Islam* is, in several instances, not that most commonly used in English-language books; simply to use the *Encyclopaedia of Islam* system here would perhaps foster further confusion when readers consult other texts or when they try to correlate what is in this book with what they already know. This book, therefore, follows the system employed in the new edition of the *Encyclopaedia of Islam* except for the letter 'j' (*jim*) and 'q' (*qaf*). For 'j' the Encyclopaedia uses 'dj', so that an entry for *hajj* (pilgrimage) will be found under *hadjdj*, for example. For 'q' the Encyclopaedia uses 'k' with a subscript dot, thus intertwining the entries with 'k' representing the letter *kaf*. The reader must remember that where 'q' is found in an Arabic word in this book, the Encyclopedia entry will have a 'k': *Qur'an* will thus be found as *Kur'an*.

In common with the practice in religious studies, all dates are cited according to the 'Common Era' (CE), numerically equivalent to Christian AD.

Introduction

Manisa, Turkey, May 1989: I lie awake in my room in the Arma Hotel, 4.30 a.m., hearing the call to prayer blaring from loudspeakers atop the minaret of a mosque a few hundred metres from my window. Other mosques start to chime in, creating a cacophony of Turkish-pronounced Arabic. A few moments later, the town is quiet again, resting until the bustle of cars, motorcycles and buses start ferrying people back and forth to school and work at 8 a.m.

The next call to prayer comes at about 1 p.m., then 5, then 8, then the cycle is completed at 10 p.m. As Muslims have frequently pointed out, it is a rhythm which punctuates the day into segments. But, I am led to observe, the timing of the prayers reflects an agricultural rhythm: farmers head out to the fields after morning prayer in the cool of the day, and finish their work as the heat of the day becomes oppressive around noon, in time for the second prayer. The rest of the day, spent at home, in the chai shop or wherever, is restful and celebrated by regular prayer times until night has descended.

The traditional religious practices fit within the traditional daily working life. The modern world has a different rhythm, however. Factories, offices and schools have oriented themselves to the 8 a.m. to 5 p.m. schedule of life. The times of prayer, it would seem, are no longer an integral part of the day's activities.

RESPONSES TO THE SITUATION

This, in a rather mundane example, is the dilemma of modern times, one easily observable by anyone who travels to the Muslim world. Traditional practices no longer 'make sense' in the context of modern life. And this leads a large number of people to abandon many of their traditional religious observances. Such a situation is what modern Muslim thinkers – those who value their tradition and wish to see it continue into the future – consider to be something that they must tackle. It is their approach to the problems and their solutions that this book will examine.

While such issues are far more complex than the following might suggest, it may be a good idea to provide an overview of the types of responses that these situations might provoke in the specific instance of the Muslim ritual prayer:

1 It may be suggested that there is no problem; the rhythm of life is not the important factor in determining the times of prayer. Rather, prayer has been dictated by God for certain times and simply must be done. Those who wish to be Muslims must perform the prayer at the appropriate times regardless. This is a fully traditional answer, where the impact of the modern world is seen as having no effect upon Islam.

2 It may be suggested that the problem lies not with the times of prayer but with modern life. Schools, offices and factories should return to the Islamic way of life and regulate their hours by prayer times. This, and many variations to it, is often described as the Fundamentalist approach.

3 It may be suggested that modern life makes demands on Islam and Islam should change. The times of prayer are not the important issue at all, but rather the attitude towards and the remembrance of God, and that can be enacted at any time. New times of prayer, if the general Muslim community could agree to them, should be instituted in keeping with the modern world. This response (which it must be admitted is rarely if ever articulated, but might be seen as implicit in certain positions) may be described as Radical Modernist.

Overall, it is the perceived inaction of the vast majority of the Muslim population which the most ardent thinkers feel they must challenge: this is the most serious threat of the modern world according to many perceptions. The modern world is simply disruptive to life, but many people seem willing to put up with that disruptiveness. Others, however, are not and it is their voices to which we will pay attention.

THE AIMS OF THIS BOOK

The period of Islam which provides the focus of interest for this book commences in the nineteenth century, perhaps as early as 1798 with the French occupation of Egypt.

In 1798 Napoleon landed in Egypt, ostensibly to protect French merchants there from local misrule, but more especially as a base of operations against the British in India. The Egyptian Mamluk troops were helpless against him, having maintained still less than other Ottoman troops an awareness of modern military developments. The population generally was likewise relatively parochial in outlook. The French set up as much as they could of the apparatus of the Enlightenment on Egyptian soil: modern hospitals, impersonal administration, scientific laboratories (they set about, among other things, recording in scientific detail the non-technicalized ways still prevailing, which were presumed about to vanish before modern French civilization); they invited the astonished local savants to inspect the show and acknowledge the moral superiority of the Revolution – claimed to be true Islam.[1]

It was at this point that the Middle East (and other parts of the world of course) faced a technologically advanced and expansionist Europe. To explore further what characterizes this modern period will be the task of Part I of this book.

Part II looks at the variety of Muslim responses to this situation. It attempts to classify those responses and provides an overview of the general intellectual trends manifested during the past two centuries.

However, the main concern of this book is not so much to delineate various Muslim positions as to come to an understanding of the approaches and solutions proposed to the situation of Islam in the modern world. An attempt is made to deal with the fundamental intellectual issues which Muslims feel that they must confront today. If there is one thing I would like this book to accomplish, it is to dispel the notion that seems implicit in the modern media treatment of Islam, especially of the religion in its fundamentalist guise, that it is not possible to be an intelligent, thinking person and a Muslim at the same time. Parts III and IV of this book deal with the very basic issues which provide both the source of identity for Islam and the source of conflict in the modern world: the figure of Muhammad and the Qur'anic scripture. These are the prime elements of the religious beliefs of all Muslims and a point of view on these elements, their status and their relative importance underlies, at least implicitly, every Muslim attempt to articulate a meaning of Islam. By looking at the views expressed over the past two centuries, the significance of the issues and the various positions taken on them are both exposed and put into historical perspective.

Another aim of this book is to say something of what it means to be a Muslim in the modern world, that is, of the practice of Islam today. There is one central question: how are the values and the demands of Islam enacted within the modern context? Analysing this problem is the task of Part V of the book and it is undertaken through attention to two disparate but central elements. First, emerging directly from some of the most controversial stances in terms of the basic sources of Islam discussed in Parts III and IV, comes the discussion of women and their place in the formation of modern

Islam. Second, as an attempt to show how the more abstract discussions spoken of in the earlier parts of the book have their ramifications in very basic issues, attention is paid to the five ritual elements of Islam and the discussions and interpretations which take place around them in the modern context.

In dealing with these topics, the Middle East region of the world is of central interest, although reference will also be made to people and ideas emanating from the Indian subcontinent, Malaysia, North America and Europe. Islam in the contemporary world does not mean the Arab world alone, although the sense in which modern Islamic nations look to the Arab world for leadership in intellectual, political and economic spheres must be acknowledged. Furthermore, the role of the Arabic language as the *lingua franca* for discussions of Islam and for the enunciation of the classical Islamic vision (to which some contemporary spokespeople make frequent reference, in both positive and negative ways) certainly argues for an emphasis on the Arab world in coming to an understanding of the intellectual vision of Islam in today's world.

THE FOUNDATIONS OF ISLAM

Many of the discussions undertaken by modern Muslims in the search for their own understanding of the role of Islam in the world presuppose a great deal about the intellectual and political fomentations which took place during the formative period of Islam. The reader of this book will, therefore, gain more insight into the subject if he or she comes to it with some basic understanding of the structures of Islam as provided, for example, in the first volume. However, this is not essential. In certain places I have supplemented the material presented in this volume with information from Volume 1 where it has seemed absolutely necessary for understanding the issues at stake.

Still, a rapid summary of the basic facts about Islam may be of some assistance. Islam, as the religion of the people known as Muslims, was revealed by God, the same God who revealed himself to the Jews and the Christians; he is known in Arabic as Allah. He revealed his religion to a native of the Hijaz on the western side of the Arabian peninsula by the name of Muhammad ibn 'Abd Allah, in the beginning of the seventh century CE. Over a period of twenty-two years, a scripture which is called the Qur'an (= Koran) was revealed to Muhammad by God. A work roughly the same length as the New Testament, the book calls on polytheists along with the Jews and the Christians to declare and put into action their commitment to God's final revealed religion. Heaven awaits those who heed the call, a fiery damnation in hell those who ignore it. Clearly it is a message which fits within the overall Judaeo-Christian tradition and, at the same time, is one which sees the whole world as eventually having to respond one way or the other to its call. As the person to whom this religion was revealed, Muhammad is considered to have had a perfect understanding of the meaning of the message. Thus, everything which he did in his life is worthy of emulation by his followers, being the perfect expression of the will of God for humanity. Those who follow (or 'submit to', as the word *muslim* suggests in its root meaning) this path of Islam form the *umma*, the community of Muslims whose common bond in religion symbolically reflects the central Islamic concept of the unity of the Divine.

METHODOLOGY IN THE STUDY OF MODERN ISLAM

Previous scholars have warned wisely about the dangers of approaching a subject such as modern Islam: 'the present religious attitudes ... [are the] least-studied and [the] most treacherous field', said H.A.R. Gibb;[2] Kenneth Cragg suggests that

> The paucity of studies has been corrected somewhat since 1945 [when Gibb was writing his book]. But the need for caution remains. Generalized judgements about an entity as manifold as modern Islam from Indonesia to Morocco, in a time so turbulent as this century, must be suitably modest and tentative.[3]

But there is far more to the problem than the vastness of the field and trying to get a grip on the subject, although those two factors should by no means be downplayed. The study of modern Islam raises severe methodological issues. These are problems of a different nature from those encountered in studying the historical past of the formative period of Islam which were reflected upon in the first volume of this book. Availability of contemporaneous sources is not the problem; as it is for the study of earlier times. Rather, it is the perspective with which we as observers approach the subject and which the sources themselves display that provides the focal point for methodological dispute.[4]

Simply put, the main issue concerns ideological biases inherent in much analysis of the contemporary period. The tendency is to see the entire world as centred on developments in Europe, as if the rest of the world had no significant existence prior to and independent of Europeans or has been irrelevant to the creation of what modern Europe is now. It is an important corrective to keep in mind that the transformation of European society over the last five centuries is not the culmination of a linear line from ancient Greece and Rome to modern France and Germany, but the result of the interplay of general human history.

Most certainly, a transformation of European society did take place between the late 1500s and the late 1700s. It was capped by two significant changes: the Industrial Revolution, ushering in the technological age, and the French Revolution, which altered basic social values. This transformation affected not only Europe, but the rest of the world as well, especially through the rise of European colonial expansion. However, one should not think that everything which has happened in the Muslim world and elsewhere during this period is simply a response to those changes on the 'outside': the Muslim world continues on its own path of organic growth and change which interacts with the rest of the world. Change is very much a two-way street.

One area which proves a great stumbling block in the study of modern Islam is the implicit (and even on occasion explicit) moral valuation of progress as it has manifested itself in the West through the transformations of the technological age. Countries which have benefited most from progress are seen to be 'more advanced' or 'better' than those which have not. However, while various useful changes in human life have come about, not all changes may be championed as necessarily good. Certainly some of them may well be thought of in this mode – modern medical advances and the eradication of smallpox, for example – but a facile judgement of the state of modern progress in one society versus another does not satisfy the demands of careful scholarship nor the understanding of human societies in their multiplicity.

The terms 'traditional' and 'modern' are a part of this value-laden system in common parlance, where 'traditional' stands for the irrational, non-scientific world view, and 'modern' for everything which opposes that. But it is possible to use these terms meaningfully, if it is carefully done. 'Traditional' refers to taking the attitude that one is doing things in the way in which they have always been done, that is, looking to the past for authority on a given matter. 'Modern' then becomes identified with the technological age, not necessarily more rational than the traditional way, but with a different view of the past, the authority of which has been displaced. The trouble is that the division is not as clear as such a definitional stance wishes to pretend. There is a tendency to assume a process of evolution from traditional to modern, but, in fact, the situation is in far more of a flux. The traditional world deals with change by rejecting or subtly altering its inherited conceptions (and thus the traditional world most assuredly does change), while the modern world never frees itself totally from the authority of the past. The modern aspects of a society are generally seen as following along hand-in-hand with its traditional ones. In sum, one might say that the terms are, at best, generalizations and that they do not reflect the realities of life as it is lived but are intellectual abstractions which can, if used reflectively, aid understanding. 'Modern' refers to the embracing of the technological aspects of contemporary society, that being understood in the broadest manner; 'traditional' does not mean the rejection of the modern but the continuation in certain aspects of life in a mode authorized by the past, notably in areas of life where other people have changed to a modern view.

The methodological dilemma is further confused by the fact that many nineteenth- and twentieth-century Muslim spokesmen (and there have been, until more recent times, very few spokeswomen) adopted the chauvinistic European mode of understanding the world: that the highlight of world existence is, in fact, in the West, that the rest of the world had to evolve and progress to that level, and that the Islamic world had been unchanging since the rise of the Mongols in the twelfth century. Time and again in reading Muslim sources this kind of apologetic, which accepts the European perspective on the question, is encountered. So, methodologically, we become even further tangled. We wish to understand contemporary Muslim world views and to do so we must recognize the cultural biases with which we approach the subject. Yet those biases are precisely what much of the material is interacting with, responding to and even adopting. And that is, in fact, what we are interested in: how modern Muslims have constructed their world views.

Part I

The contemporary world and the phenomenon of modernity

1 Describing the contemporary world

THE PHENOMENON OF MODERNITY

The real challenge that the Muslim society has had to face and is still facing is at the level of social institutions and social ethic as such. And the real nature of this crisis is not the fact that the Muslim social institutions in the past have been wrong or irrational but the fact that there has been a social system at all which now needs to be modified and adjusted. This social system has, in fact, been perfectly rational in the past, i.e. it has been working perfectly well, as perfectly well as any other social system. The disadvantage of the Muslim society at the present juncture is that whereas in the early centuries of development of social institutions in Islam, Islam started from a clean slate, as it were, and had to carve out *ab initio* a social fabric – an activity of which the product was the medieval social system – now, when Muslims have to face a situation of fundamental rethinking and reconstruction, their acute problem is precisely to determine how far to render the slate clean again and on what principles and by what methods, in order to create a new set of institutions.[1]

While Fazlur Rahman, the author of the above passage, is enunciating a particular position within the modernist Muslim debate, he strikes a central point common to all who try to contemplate the relevance of Islam today by speaking of a modern situation of 'fundamental rethinking and reconstruction' in which Islam now finds itself. But before tackling the proposed answers to that question something more fundamental must first be approached: why and how has this situation of 'fundamental rethinking and reconstruction' arisen? What are the characteristics of the modern age which have created this situation? Why has Islam had to face them? And why does facing them seem to be such a problem?

What are the characteristics of this thing we call the 'modern era'?

There are many ways of analysing the idea called 'modernity'. At its simplest level, it might be said that modernity is that which renders the past problematic. Notably (and this is what makes this definition so significant), once tradition – the past – has been questioned and examined, there is no going back. The ideas of the past (for example, in terms of historical facts) can never have the same weight again, even if the challenge of modernity is ultimately rejected.[2]

Modernity is that which has created fundamental changes in behaviour and belief about economics, politics, social organization and intellectual discourse. Once again, it is important to keep in mind that changes have happened throughout the world; this is not just a matter of Western influences on the rest of the world. Modernity must be seen as a world phenomenon.

In the economic sphere, change is seen in terms of industrialization and consequent economic growth, the formation of large capital sums, the growth of science and the emergence of new classes of people and social mobility. In the political area, it is the growth of political parties (and the belief in the moral evolution resulting from that growth), unions and youth groups. In the social dimension, the change in relations between the sexes (with its economic implications), mass communications, urbanization, travel and generally increased mobility are especially marked. In the intellectual realm, the prominence of the idea of progress, the emergence of secular-rational norms and the rise of historical studies[3] all make the phenomenon of change apparent. All of this has brought with it, or brought about as a consequence, a change in the historical reality in which we live.

The five pillars of modernity

Many attempts have been made to try to define more closely the characteristics of the modern period in order to say just how it is different from past eras. Peter Berger's 'Toward a Critique of Modernity'[4] has become a classic statement of such a definition. He speaks of five 'dilemmas of modernity':

1 Abstraction (in the way life confronts bureaucracy and technology especially).
2 Futurity (the future as the primary orientation for activity and the imagination, and life governed by the clock).
3 Individuation (the separation of the individual from any sense of a collective entity, thus producing alienation).
4 Liberation (life viewed as dominated by choice and not fate; 'things could be other than what they have been').
5 Secularization (the massive threat to the plausibility of religious belief).

Harvey Cox[5] has modified these into a slightly more positive form and speaks of the aptly named (for this context) 'five pillars of modernity'. The modern period is said to be characterized by the following aspects:

1 The emergence of sovereign national states as legally defined entities in a global political system, most of which have emerged in their present form at most 200 years ago.
2 Science-based technology as a principal source of images for life and its possibilities.
3 Bureaucratic rationalism as a way of organizing and administering human thought and activity, where institutions take on their own intellectual life, producing people who feel alienated, powerless and apathetic ('I only work here').
4 The quest for profit maximization as a means to motivate work and distribute goods and services (thus within both capitalism and socialism) as manifested in, for example, the capitalist mode of production and marketing.
5 Secularization and trivialization of religion and the use of the spiritual for profane purposes, manifested in the removal of religion's concern with politics and economics.

Secularization needs further comment, given the context of our investigation. This concept may be defined[6] as the process of emancipation of certain areas of social, cultural and political life from the dominance or control of traditional religious ideas; it has been both a contributing factor in modernization and a result of it. The terms used to describe the modern era – enlightened, secular, rational, disenchanted (i.e. the loss of magic), scientific, post-traditional – all indicate the tendency of secularization.

In fact, the attitudes towards religion are central elements of what many people identify as modern, at least in popular parlance. For example, the demolition of the truth of the Bible, the rejection of the divinity of Jesus, and the doubts expressed about the value of much that has been taught for generations are the most obvious such elements within Christianity.[7] But these are negative elements, matters which have created fear and terror along with an almost perverse attraction to this modern age. To put this somewhat more positively, one may speak of the modern age as coinciding with the emergence of the philosophical principle of the self as the judge on matters of truth and validity: Descartes' 'I think therefore I am' remains the only basic certain truth as opposed to traditional religious values and their claims to eternal validity.

Some observers have noted that this tendency towards secularization especially, along with the other aspects of modernity, happened in Europe initially but have become of crucial significance for the rest of the world.

Therefore, European religion – Christianity – has had to respond to this situation from the beginning of the age of industrialization, and the ways in which it has done so have become paradigmatic (at least to some extent) for other religions. To a degree, this would appear to be intrinsically true, but it is also a position urged by some writers: that Muslims should learn from the Christian experience and be prepared to relinquish certain aspects of their traditional faith while maintaining others. This kind of writing about Islam especially has received a great deal of criticism recently[8] but continues nevertheless.[9]

Other people, perhaps with a greater political (rather than religious) orientation towards life, have isolated another series of adjectives which characterize the modern period: colonial, imperialist, missionary, Western invasion. There can be no doubt that isolating such elements is important in understanding the perceptions of the modern period in the Muslim world. This view, however, tends to see the modern world in terms of confrontation between the West and the Islamic world; other people may wish to subsume these elements under broader categories, however, such as the world-wide emergence of national states. Still, the reality of this perception cannot be underplayed.

CHARACTERISTICS OF THE MODERN ERA IN THE MUSLIM WORLD

How has modernity made its impact on the Muslim world? The sense of the tension created in the modern context is one of the first things which strikes many travellers, and it may be seen in many films and other media portrayals: the absurd and distressing confrontation between modern and ancient ways of life. Donkeys are still vying for a place on the road as decrepit cars and trucks, amid the Mercedes, go whizzing by; the importation of the McDonalds–Coca-Cola consumer culture exists in the face of vast wealth and abject poverty without the build-up period of time which North American and European society had to adjust itself to that consumerism. Consumer society 'is at odds with the pre-take-off stage of the Middle Eastern economy, creating new needs and raising expectations that the economy cannot deliver'.[10] This becomes a powerful fundamentalist argument against the West, for appealing to Western values and aspirations is seen to be the cause of contemporary frustrations.

Yet the Muslim world has in certain ways adapted to the modern world through the use of its ancient resources; these have proven a source of strength as well as a source of tension. The utilization and re-utilization of modern materials – the implicit rejection of the throw-away society and the planned obsolescence of the West – are frequently startling and encouraging to the observer accustomed to North American-style consumerism.

The impact of modernity on the Islamic world is characterized as having a number of factors; these have been isolated by those living in the Muslim world as well as by outside observers. Yvonne Haddad,[11] for example, speaks of three major factors: the cycle of ascendancy and decline, the impact of the nationalist and socialist challenge, and Zionism; others may easily be added to that list.

Ascendancy and decline

With the rise of European and American power in the world, the Islamic world along with the rest of the Third World – a term indicative in itself of the basic issue – has found itself subjugated politically and exploited economically. A recognition of impotence in the face of this newly emerged power along with a shared memory of a powerful past has produced a great deal of soul searching and analysis. What are the reasons for this decline into subjugation and exploitation? The answers have frequently been religious, a response fostered and encouraged by negative post-Enlightenment attitudes towards religion in general and towards Islam in particular.

Haunting all of the discussions within the Muslim world is the notion of the failure of Islam. Has Islam somehow fallen by the wayside, become unable to cope with the emerging world and the contemporary human situation? This, of course, is a shattering thought for any religion, but it is especially so for Islam because the idea of success in the world has been central to Islamic ideology from the very early period of Islam. Acting as a paradigm for later Islamic thinking, Muhammad is pictured as moving from Mecca to Medina (the *hijra*) in the midst of his preaching career in order to be successful. Islam would not have been revealed to the world, as God's last statement, if it were not divinely pre-ordained to succeed. God's word cannot be frustrated by human obstinacy. Islamic history and the golden age of Islam, in the same time period as the dark ages of Europe, only reinforce the notion of the success of the religion in further, very tangible terms. The rise of Europe as a colonialist power, therefore, shattered a deeply held Muslim idea – even, it might be said, one of the basic presuppositions of Islamic existence. A crisis of identity faced those who did not get carried away on the Western bandwagon and who wished to investigate the roots of the problem. The modern situation was perceived to be one of fundamental challenge to Islam, therefore; the failure to be able to respond would be the failure of Islam as a religion. What then is the status of Islam when it is not in political ascendancy in the world?

The answers to this problem have been varied, as the rest of this book will display: the extent to which Islam itself might be seen as the cause of the gradual decline of its civilization is, in part, the subject of debate. Is it Islam itself which needs modification in the modern world or is it Muslims who have not lived up to the demands of Islam, so that consequently the civilization has declined? This question arises most frequently in discussions over science and technology. The failure to embrace modern science (which, it is often argued, stems from Muslim medieval advances) along with the scientific mentality as embodied in the Western educational system is the cause of Islam's decline according to some. Others, however, would say that it is faith in God which is more crucial than the technology itself and thus they reject this entire argument.

Nationalism and socialism

Modern political ideologies have been seen by some as a way out of the present dilemma of decline but also as an attractive modern option in and by themselves. Socialism especially has attracted attention both as an alternative to Islam and as a way to construct an entirely new society. But it has also been seen as the true embodiment of Islamic principles, especially in aspects of equality and social justice and as being against Western capitalism. In this view, Muhammad established socialist principles in his state, which means that such a structure of society should take precedence over capitalism. After the period of occupation by European nations, democracy as a system of government, in the argument of many people, has lost its glamour and its moral claim to supremacy. Yet the civic virtues of Europe still hold their appeal for many. The impact of more recent developments – the collapse of the colonial empires – has resulted in further confusion in the overall picture. The emergence of new political states, areas which formerly had little unified identity in many cases, has fostered the new phenomenon of nationalism in ethnic and/or cultural terms which often do not include Islam, at least not as that religion has been classically portrayed. Events in 1991 in Iraq and the Kurdish rebellion indicate the strength of such issues. This indicates that there have been significant changes in traditional, pre-modern loyalty patterns brought about by nationalism.[12]

Zionism

Zionism has led to a strengthening of Islamic identity according to many observers, although most would also comment that, even so, no united front has appeared among the Islamic nations, especially the Arabs. The sense that the existence of Israel represents the absolute trough of the decline of Muslim civilization is felt by many: whether Israel is perceived as a punishment for Muslim errors in the past or as a part of a continued Western presence in the Middle East, the insult that the nation represents to the

Muslim world cannot be overestimated. Some people have argued that Israel's success as a nation – economically, politically – is evidence of the need to adopt Western ways. But for the most part, many feel that Israel represents further evidence of the sinful ways of Muslims and the need for a purification of Islam. The 1967 war between Israel and the Arab world deeply affected the collective psyche of the Muslim people in the wake of the defeat of the Arab troops.[13] The rise of fundamentalist movements, a renewed interest in the symbolic role of Jerusalem and a host of other factors are frequently attributed to this war.

Oil

Another very specific issue may be added to this list of ways in which modernity has impacted upon the Muslim world. Oil revenues have produced an ambivalence similar to that caused by the existence of Israel: they are either a curse or a blessing, according to the perspective taken. The impact of the vast revenues has been to take Muslims away from Islam, to the point that Saudi Arabia is frequently pictured as the most corrupt and un-Islamic nation in the world, a land of wine-drinking multimillionaires who repress the less fortunate citizens of their own country and do nothing to enhance Islam. The Iraqi invasion of Kuwait and the various justifications which have emerged for it, especially as revealed in statements from Muslims outside the Arab countries, echo this sentiment to a great extent. The opposite argument, that oil revenues now put the population of the Muslim world in a position of affecting the world, giving them the possibility of standing up for their own rights and permitting the propagation of Islam within the context of the modern world, is frequently made: oil revenues are a gift from God to allow the Muslim world to function in the modern context.[14] The impact of oil is, of course, only a part of the whole discussion of the modern industrial-technological civilization and its impact.

Other factors

Emmanuel Sivan[15] speaks of television as the most obvious and blatant symbol of the invasion of the modern world and the most effective tool in its propagation. The loose morality, the instant gratification, life as centred on love and pleasure while oblivious to religious beliefs are all a part of the Hollywood image which is bringing the Islamic world into the global village.[16] Other points may be raised: education makes no attempt to relate the modern scientific world to Islam, the modern family is reinforced as against the traditional, and nationalism is reinforced as against the concept of the Islamic community. Of course, this analysis of society and its ills is by no means unique to Islam: witness Allan Bloom in his *The Closing of the American Mind*:

> Classical music is dead among the young. . . . Classical music is now a special taste, like Greek language or pre-Columbian archeology, not a common culture of reciprocal communication and psychological short-hand. Thirty years ago, most middle-class families made some of the old European music a part of the home, partly because they liked it, partly because they thought it was good for the kids. . . . But rock music has one appeal only, a barbaric appeal, to sexual desire – not love, not *eros*, but sexual desire undeveloped and untutored. . . . The inevitable corollary of such sexual interest is rebellion against the parental authority that represses it.[17]

These perceptions are by no means unique and, with their own cultural forms and their own socio-cultural assumptions, these same sentiments are echoed by certain segments of the population throughout the world.

Clifford Geertz has said,

> [In face of the modern world, people] lose their sensibility. Or they channel it into ideological fervor. Or they adopt an imported creed. Or they turn worriedly in upon themselves. Or they cling even more intensely to the faltering traditions. Or they try to rework those traditions into more effective forms. Or they split themselves in half, living spiritually in the past and physically in the present. Or they try to express their religious-ness in secular activities. And a few simply fail to notice their world is moving or, noticing, just collapse.[18]

THE ROLE OF ISLAM IN THE MODERN WORLD

One basic point needs to be made in understanding the various discussions which relate to the role Islam should or could (or should not and could not) play in the modern world. Religion, and Islam specifically, is classically thought of as the element which provides the grounding for an individual's life, the interpretative core through which life's experiences may be understood. But the past-oriented nature of religion as it acts to preserve that grounding has meant that its role in the contemporary period has been problematic. The question becomes one of what form Islam should present to the world in order to take its place in modern society.

As has already been suggested, much of the character of the modern period could be termed the impact of secularism upon a traditional religious system; in that way, the threat to Islam is the same as that posed to Judaism and Christianity. Whether Islam is viable in the modern world is the question, especially since Islam has classically been conceived (if not always manifested in history) as a politicized religion. The reality of the matter is that, in the modern context, politicization is even further distant than it was in medieval times. In those ancient times, at least the presence of the caliph as a religio-political authority figure was maintained, even if that person was in fact powerless in front of the military rulers and the independent scholarly elite. The office of the caliphate was officially eliminated with the rise of Republican Turkey in 1924. The perception of some Muslims in the modern period is that the impact of secularization is thus attacking the heart of Islam at its theoretical basis.

Islam is the civilizational basis of the Muslim world in politics, in society, in life. In modern terminology, it provides the linguistic basis by which life is experienced, delimits how things are to be perceived and sets the limits to discourse.[19] Can Islam continue with this role in the modern world? Should it even try to? These are the fundamental questions which some Muslims have chosen to face, and continue to face. It is the nature of religion in and by itself which has rendered the questions so difficult.

Some would say that it is the traditional nature of religion as it is manifested in its attitude to authority, based upon a notion of sacredness, and which sees authority as stemming from the past in a continuous flow up to the present, that jars so much with the modern ethos. A value is placed on the past because it supports the authority which exists today. But modernity, as we have seen, involves rapid and multi-faceted change. Religions have always had to face changing circumstances and they have developed a number of mechanisms by which this is handled. New ideas, whether emergent, borrowed or acquired, are legitimated in a number of paradigmatic ways: change is seen as a legitimate unfolding of the past; new ideas are proven to have been present always; new ideas are proven to have legitimacy through a claim that they should have been present, but the faithful have ignored/suppressed them so that a more legitimate continuity with tradition is discovered through change; or new ideas are accepted through a cultural revolution, the most radical of all strategies.

Under the impact of the rapid change which the modern world has inflicted, many Muslims have experienced a severe weakening of the traditional conception of the eternal, unchanging Muslim legal code, the *shari'a*. At the same time, it is within the *shari'a* that various strategies have been employed in order to try to face the challenge of change. The Muslim law had been firmly established by the great jurists of the past (it has classically been seen as the greatest accomplishment of medieval scholastic Islam). Within the traditional framework, there is room for interpretation and modification, but there cannot be a questioning of the nature and the basis of the authority and the relevance of the law. How to assess the law today then, in light of those characteristics of modernity suggested above, has proven to be a challenge, to say the least. This is especially a problem because of the range of topics covered by the *shari'a*: while matters such as politics and taxation remained only theoretically under the guidance of the religious code in medieval Islam, areas of personal law – marriage, divorce, inheritance – were the stronghold of religion.[20] It is, however, precisely in many of those areas that the contemporary world has effected a great deal of change and where the pressures, especially of nineteenth-century European values, have been felt the most. Equally problematic has been the fact that during the nineteenth century (if not earlier) most Islamic states either adopted or had imposed upon them European law codes which simply displaced the traditional *shari'a*. This process provided a means by which to introduce reforms, for example in areas of women's and family rights, but the result has been that those who wished to see religion continue to play a significant role in their societies had either to demonstrate that their religion, in fact, supported the reforms (and this became the position of those commonly termed the Modernists) or to demand that the secular law codes be repealed and simply replaced by Islamic ones (a stance characteristic of more conservative elements).

The response of modern Muslims to this situation has indeed been of every conceivable type, as the rest of this book will demonstrate. For some, the solution to the question of the role of Islam today is found in Islamic 'totalism': that Islam should govern every part of life, from politics to personal conduct to scientific investigation. At the other end of the spectrum, some have argued that the former Muslim ideal of a religio-political mix is the main stumbling block to the modernization of Islam, itself a desirable aim; religion should be a personal, interior matter, an issue between the believer and God and only in that way will Islam remain a vital force in today's world. In between these two responses remains a variety of compromise solutions and non-solutions which support an unintegrated mode of existence.

THE POST-MODERN PHENOMENON AND THE QUAINTNESS OF MODERNISTS

For those on the outside, however, the Muslim discussion of this confrontation with the modern period, as described in the previous sections, often seems rather quaint. The arguments still seem to revolve around the relevance or danger of Darwin, Marx and Freud, as if those figures represent the state of Western thinking.

There is little evidence in the Muslim world of what is called in some circles post-modernism. Certainly, radical Marxism is present and that may be viewed as a reaction within the post-modern framework; it is one, however, that calls for a total rejection of Islam and thus it can hardly be termed an Islamic post-modern ideology.[21] The post-modern questioning of the basic presuppositions of religion within a religious framework – the structures of authority, its orientation to the past, its fixation on success – is extremely limited.

What describes the post-modern age?

Furthermore, to some people, the descriptions given above of what characterizes the modern world are woefully inadequate. The world has already entered a new period of challenge.

Mass communications have made the existence of independent states anachronistic; a world community is emerging but its character is extremely unclear.[22] Recognition has come about of the limits to progress in science and the impact that faith in science has had on the world; the perception of an ecological crisis is a large part of this. The recognition of the threat of technology has raised questions of whether just because something can be done, it should be done. Despite earlier optimism, technology has not managed to solve the basic problems of the world such as starvation. Faith in the moral evolution of humanity (especially the trust in democracy) has been destroyed in the furnaces of Auschwitz; the reality of continuing racism and of the potential for evil that lurks in humanity is felt. The impact of the industrialization of the world in terms of unemployment, pollution, mal-distribution of goods and the merging of cultures has been recognized. Feminism and the assertiveness of less-developed countries (with a view to directing their own future through their own value systems) have both accompanied and perhaps been precipitated by post-modernism. These issues are manifested in general terms by the post-modern realization of the powerlessness of the individual to effect change on what have become living institutions.[23] To paraphrase the words of Harvey Cox, if the problem of modernism is termed 'we cannot pray', the problem of post-modernism is 'we cannot (and others cannot) eat'. Post-modernism entails confrontation with the social issues of the day, here conceived within a religious framework such as feminism, peace and war, minority expressions of theology, political stances, and economics.

The most radical modernizers: the 'destroyers of Islam'?

Whether the post-modern situation is taken seriously is one of the differentiating factors in trends in modern thought in general. Fundamentalism tends not to confront the reality of the situation; it proposes in its crasser forms, for example, that homeless people are those who simply choose to live that way. The emergence of critical theology in Christian and Jewish circles is marked by a willingness to confront the post-modern condition seriously.

To the extent that Muslim post-modernism does exist, its greatest manifestation is to be found outside the cultural sphere of the Muslim countries themselves. The future may offer a different situation, in some people's estimation, with the rise of the women's movement and the inversion of power structures within the Muslim world as will be explored in Part V of this book. It is worthy of note now, however, that even here the positions enunciated seem limited: we do not see many women enunciating a new *shari'a* that displaces the male prerogative, or many who work on a theology based upon a female (or all-inclusive, gender-neutral) language.

One example of what might be called post-Modernist thought in Islam (or even 'post-Islamic', if that be understood in the same way in which 'post-Modernist' is intimately linked to 'Modernist') may help illustrate this topic, to which we shall return. Mohammed Arkoun, an Algerian living in Paris and writing primarily in French, provides the most vivid example.

Arkoun poses the question in an essay written as an introduction to a translation of the Qur'an and then reprinted in his *Lectures du Coran*: 'How should the Qur'an be read?' with an emphasis on the the idea of 'How should it be read today?'[24] This is not a question commonly posed in the Muslim framework and reveals immediately Arkoun's concerns. The point is one not really of simply how to read it, but of how to understand the book in the light of modern intellectual thought. The problem is, as the Christian post-modern theologian Mark C. Taylor expresses it:

> [T]he 'texts' that have guided and grounded previous generations often appear illegible in the modern and postmodern worlds. Instead of expressing a single story or coherent plot, human lives tend to be inscribed in multiple and often contradictory texts. What makes sense and is meaningful in one situation frequently seems senseless and meaningless in another setting. The resulting conflict creates confusion that extends far beyond the pages of the book.[25]

How, then, is one to retrieve the Qur'an both from the mountains of learned philological knowledge and from the literalist tendencies of many modern Islamic movements, and to discover something which speaks to the modern, intelligent individual? As Arkoun suggests, the task is one that is already under way in Judaism and Christianity but is still to be confronted in the Islamic context. It means coming to an understanding of the social and historical conditioning of all human existence, including language, leading to a liberation from the categories of thought imposed by past places and eras. This is not simply a study of history, because that discipline, in much of its Orientalist manifestation, is still deeply entrenched in the nineteenth-century notion of a search for absolutes and essentials. Rather, the historicity of knowledge will be discovered by the totality of the methods of the social sciences, according to Arkoun, asking questions not of 'what really happened' (in the formulation of the discipline of history) but of how it is that certain ideas came to be a part of the social imagination[26] and of the role that those ideas play in the construction of reality for society.

Regardless of one's views of Arkoun's attempts,[27] in his posing of the questions he is marked as 'post' the Modernists of Islam. However, the adverse reaction which such positions evoke amongst other enunciators of modern visions of Islam cannot be overestimated. The historicity of Islam is seen as being rejected in the attempt by Arkoun and his ilk to escape from the dualisms of religion and society; as in similar suggestions in contemporary Christian thought, such views are often termed destructive of everything which people hold dear in their religion.

Part II
Muslims and modernity

2　Islam's encounter with the contemporary world

CLASSIFICATION OF MUSLIM APPROACHES TO MODERNITY

The main issues for Islam in the contemporary situation relate to the place of religion in public life – social, economic, legal, political, intellectual. It is precisely those dimensions which are crucial to a definition of modernity and which thus create the problems to be faced. The dimensions of the phenomenon of modernity as sketched in the previous part of this book focus on the changes which have taken place in all these aspects of public life. That the focus of the conflict is found in this sphere is confirmed by the complementary principle that, to an almost complete extent, there has been no calling into question of Islam itself as a private need or mode of personal devotion, nor have there been many major attempts at a theological reformulation of the faith in the light of the modern world. Therefore, studying the reactions of Muslims to modernity is primarily a matter of addressing the question of what specific place the religion is to have in modern life rather than questioning the existence of the religion as such. Can answers to the dilemmas and problems of modern life be found in the religion? If so, how? Can religion at least provide a way to cope?

Some of the characteristics of the modern era, particularly its impact on the Muslim world, have been sketched very broadly in the previous chapter. We must now try to specify matters a little more carefully by attempting to present a schematization of responses to the modern world. Certain characteristics may be suggested quite readily which may then be expanded by means of further reflection:

1　There are those who deny all value to modernity and see it as the root cause of all modern troubles.
2　There are those who see modernity as a mixed blessing.
3　There are those who hold to a critical or modified modernism, suggesting

that the modernist project is a worthy one but that individual elements must be assessed carefully.
4 There are those who attempt to go outside Islam, for example the Ahmadiyya, the Baha'is, and atheists or agnostics.

A SIMPLE CATEGORIZATION

A tri-part division of religious ways of interacting with the modern age is suggested by many analyses and ties in with the above listed characteristics: Traditionalist (sometimes termed Normative or Orthodox); Fundamentalist (sometimes termed Neo-Normativist or Revivalist); and Modernist (sometimes termed Acculturating or Modernizing).[1] A simple, although controversial example can serve to illustrate how this sort of division works in the case of Islam: polygamy.

1 The Traditionalist group may be characterized by its acceptance of multiple-wife marriages, suggesting that to think otherwise is to accept Western standards; Islamic tradition has allowed polygamy and that is the way things should be.
2 The Modernist group would suggest a position based on the premise that men and women are equal and monogamy is morally good because it aims towards a concept of social welfare, while polygamy has potentially negative effects on family life; it is often argued that the Qur'an supports this position.[2]
3 The Fundamentalist group will start from the Qur'an and say that that was aiming for monogamy all along but made allowances for ancient habits which no longer have any relevance.

It must be remembered that these are theoretical categories only; people, in the realities of their life situations, can rarely, if ever, be fitted neatly into one position or the other. The categories are heuristic, helpful to indicate tendencies but rarely adequate to constitute a full analysis. Furthermore, such categorizations do not allow for historical change within the categories themselves, as will become clear. Modernists, for example, have a substantially different face today from that they had at the turn of the twentieth century. While the characterizations of these groups, along with refinements to be added later, will be employed in subsequent parts of this volume, they are too schematic and reductive to provide structure for a full analysis. Their value lies in their ability to reflect the overall dimensions of discussions in modern Islam and thereby provide some tools for more critical analysis.

Attitude to the past in the Traditionalist group

Each of the above three categories may be said to display a different attitude towards the authority of the past. The Traditionalist group holds to the full authority of the past and that change should not and does not affect the traditions of the past. Change is to be rejected. Such an expression of the essence of the Traditionalist group is misleading, however: to some extent it falls captive to the group's own rhetoric. Islam, as a cultural entity, has, after all, always been able to cope with change and has built into its structures ways of dealing with change. New situations were ably managed by the institutionalized juridical system. Certainly it is true that the basic sources of Islam – the Qur'an and the *sunna* – are viewed as unchanging, for they are, in some manner, representations in the world of the unchanging God. But this conception, contrary to some suggestions,[3] did not curtail all reaction to changing circumstances. Rather, the issue for the Traditionalists in the contemporary period has been one of substantial challenge to well-established patterns of life and methods of legitimizing change. The Traditionalist group contains within it many of the learned scholars (*'ulama'*) who might be thought to have a vested interest in maintaining the status quo, many of the mystically oriented Sufi groups and the vast majority of those who have not been exposed to modern education and thus to a great extent have not experienced the challenge of modernity to such a degree as to consider it a personal problem.

Fundamentalist Islam and revivalism

The Fundamentalist group, in contrast to the Traditionalist, is characterized by its desire to accept change in a controlled fashion; it therefore uses the authoritative sources of the past to legitimize changes in the present day. This group has a long intellectual history in Islam, or at least that is the perception of its adherents. This is an important observation because it illustrates well the fact that modernity is not just an issue of Islam facing the onslaught of the West: Islam has had its own organic growth and development and, to emphasize the point once again, has developed its own methods of coping with change in the past. That, from some people's perceptions, those methods are now being severely tried is, of course, a part of the overall internal Muslim debate.

Ibn Taymiyya, who died in 1328, is the intellectual hero of the fundamentalist tendency. He argued strenuously for purging Islam of various practices prevalent at his time, especially popular Sufi practices such as excessive asceticism, tomb visitations and saint worship, along with beliefs such as miracle working. He argued against these things by appealing to the

Qur'an and the practice (*sunna*) of Muhammad; anything which could not be justified on this basis was to be rejected. Thus, music and song were to be considered non-Islamic, for example. The entire Sufi proposal of the ecstatic experience of God was not a valid criterion by which to judge what is right and wrong (which is one of the arguments which al-Ghazzali had used a few centuries earlier to legitimate Sufi practices). Similar thoughts arose in the eighteenth century, primarily in the Arabian movement which became known as the Wahhabis, once again a movement against Sufism and Shi'ism. Led by Ibn 'Abd al-Wahhab (1703–87), the movement argued that the attitude of reverence towards saints had led to a blind acceptance of their authority and this was to be rejected and replaced by the sole authority of Islam – the Qur'an and the *sunna*. This reliance on text results in what is frequently termed literalism or fundamentalism but, at the same time, it opens up the possibilities of independent reasoning through the rejection of authority by that very process of the return to the text and the ignoring of traditional interpretation of those texts. Ibn 'Abd al-Wahhab, and much of the following Fundamentalist movement, tends towards an anti-intellectualism, especially anti-philosophy. This is perhaps one of the key points for differentiating Modernists and Fundamentalists (and, in fact, separates them from Ibn Taymiyya also).[4] Shah Wali Allah (1702–62), a mystic theologian, represents a similar tendency in the Indian context, but he placed greater emphasis on gradual reform than on the strident confrontations of Ibn 'Abd al-Wahhab.

The movements connected to Ibn 'Abd al-Wahhab and Shah Wali Allah may be termed 'pre-modern', in the sense that they developed before the impact of the industrialized West had been felt. They may best be termed 'purification' movements[5] and they certainly sowed the seeds for later social and legal change in the Islamic world. They seem to have been caused by a dissatisfaction with the more rigid formulations of medieval Islam, especially in the legal schools. The movement also picks up on a well-established tradition in Islam regarding the *mujaddid*, or renewer of the faith, believed to be an essential part of each age.[6] Fazlur Rahman has characterized these pre-Modernist groups as having the following characteristics:

i) a deep and transforming concern with the socio-moral degeneration of Muslim society; ii) a call to 'go back' to original Islam and shed the superstitions inculcated by popular forms of Sufism, to get rid of the idea of the fixity and finality of the traditional schools of law, and to attempt to perform *ijtihad*, that is, to rethink for oneself the meaning of the original message; iii) a call to remove the crushing burden of a predeterministic outlook produced by popular religion but also materially contributed to by the almost ubiquitous influence of Ash'arite theology; and iv) a call to carry out this revivalist reform through armed force (*jihad*) if necessary.[7]

This is the platform which many of the Fundamentalist movements in contemporary Islam have inherited or, at least, which they look back to for inspiration and analysis.

These trends in thought are crucial to the writings of people associated with contemporary expressions of what has been termed the revival of Islam led by the Fundamentalists. Abul A'la Mawdudi is a prime example. Born in 1903, he was the founder of the Jama'at-i Islami in India in 1941 and was a major religio-political leader in Pakistan until his death in 1979. His call was for a return to the Qur'an and a purified *sunna* so that Islam might be revitalized; this could only truly happen if Islam became the constitution of the state, and this was the political goal towards which he worked in Pakistan.[8] Sayyid Qutb of Egypt provides another example. Qutb lived from 1906 to 1966 and became the intellectual spokesman for the Muslim Brotherhood. He championed a return to 'pure Islam' and a move away from the materialism of the West which he perceived as contaminating Islam. Allegiance should be to Islam alone, for that provides the perfect social system for all humanity, one which will cure all the ills of the modern world. Once a truly Islamic state is established, all aspects of life will fall into their proper place.[9] Both of these thinkers will be dealt with in later parts of this book.

Islamic modernism and its history

The Modernist group has seen greater advantage to be found within the modern circumstance by embracing change and making religion itself subject to change. The Modernist position is frequently based upon a principle of differentiating basic moral precepts from specific legal prescriptions. This movement too has had a substantial history. It developed in the nineteenth century with people such as Jamal al-Din al-Afghani (1839–97),[10] Muhammad 'Abduh (1849–1905) and Rashid Rida (1865–1935) in Egypt, and Sayyid Ahmad Khan (1817–98) and Muhammad Iqbal (1876–1938) in India. Al-Afghani is famous for his idea of Pan-Islamism, which he saw as a way of reviving and uniting Islam against Europe; this idea was to be combined with an embracing of philosophy and science which, he argued, transcend particular communities. He greatly influenced 'Abduh, and through him Rida, who worked further to synthesize those features of the West which seemed desirable (especially its scientific rationality) with the essential truths of Islam. The situation in India was very similar. Ahmad Khan argued that modern knowledge and the use of reason was required in order to bring vitality back to Islam. Essentially this involved a separation between Islam, as a religion of ritual and law, and reason or science, which was not seen to be under the control of religious law although it was in keeping with the true principles of the faith itself. Deep down, the argument went, there was no conflict between Islam and modernity, for they functioned on different planes. Islamic law is not fixed but must change in each situation, especially in the social realm. Iqbal's message, frequently couched in mystically inspired poetry, urged the same return to the essentials of Islam, to be found in its true sources.

Reconstruction, *islah*, became the catchword for this trend.[11] As a movement it may also be seen to have had a substantial influence on Fundamentalists as well, with its call of 'back to the sources'. But its emphasis on elements of the West as having some value for Islamic culture (as opposed to the self-sufficiency of Islam), and its tendency towards a definition of religion centred on the individual in his or her relationship with God, along with its flexible attitude towards the social aspect of the faith, mark the Modernists as distinct. A number of factors may be isolated as contributing to the rise of the Modernists, which illustrates once again that speaking simply of modernism as a reaction to Europe does not represent an accurate summary of the issues involved. According to the analysis of Ali Merad, the pressures of pre-Modernist Fundamentalism, the development of the printed word as a result of the introduction of the printing press in Arab countries around 1822, the influence of Western culture, the liberal evolution of the Ottoman regime (for example, introduction of civil liberties in 1839) and the structural renovation of the Eastern Christian churches, showing an example of 'zeal in the service of a faith', all contributed substantially to stimulating a 'renaissance', *nahda*, within the Arab countries especially which has become identified with the Modernist trend.[12]

THE MOVE OUTSIDE ISLAM

It is a common phenomenon in religion that, if the questioning of the authority of the past is taken far enough in the desire to be able to accommodate or compensate for the changes of the modern period, there is a need for a new source of authority. (This may even account for the rise of each religion in its formative period also: modernity, as such, may not be the root cause of the emergence of these movements, therefore – they may stem from a very basic dislocation in human existence.) Such an understanding can be used to characterize various offshoots of Islam in the modern period which clearly have a Modernist stance and a renewed sense of authority.

The Ahmadiyya is one such group, founded by Mirza Ghulam Ahmad

(1835–1908) and now comprising some four million members.[13] Ghulam Ahmad was educated in India with law or government service under the British in mind, but in 1877 he started devoting himself to the cause of Islam. His earliest writings aim towards a revitalization of Islam within the modernizing platform. As early as 1882, he claimed to be the *mujaddid*, 'renewer', of Islam, and by 1891 he had put forth the proclamation that he was the promised Messiah of the Muslim community. Later he suggested he was also an *avatar* of Krishna, Jesus returned to earth and the manifestation of Muhammad. He claimed to be a prophet in receipt of revelation, but one who was sent without a book of scripture or a new religion (and thus he always asserted that he was subordinate to Muhammad). His function was to return Islam to its proper formulation, by means of a prophetic-revelatory authority within a messianic-eschatological context. Debate has followed Ghulam Ahmad, dividing both his followers and the Muslim community as a whole, concerning both the extent and validity of his claims and the status of the finality of Muhammad's prophethood and revelation, doctrines which are considered central to Islam, as it has been classically defined. For our purposes here, however, it is sufficient to note that the Ahmadiyya vests authority in Ghulam Ahmad beyond that normally associated even with a *mujaddid* and that this has been done in support of a Modernist stance, embracing modern science and many moral ideals associated with the Enlightenment, in combination with a return to the essence of Islam as it is revealed in the Qur'an and through the guidance of Mirza Ghulam Ahmad. For the Ahmadiyya, the correct interpretation of Islam has been vested with the authority of revelation.

The members of the Ahmadiyya proclaim themselves to be Muslims, although in countries such as Pakistan they have been declared outside the Islamic community and in many places their missionary activity (which remains a very strong emphasis of the movement, reflecting an effort from the very beginning to counter Christian missionary activity in India, and is also associated with an active Qur'an translation programme, something generally not encouraged within more traditional circles) has raised severe worries. The situation is quite different for the Baha'is who do not wish to consider themselves Islamic but rather proclaim themselves to be members of a new 'World Faith' which supersedes Islam.

The Baha'is trace their origins to 'Ali Muhammad Shirazi (1819–50) of Iran, who referred to himself as the Bab, the 'Gate', and proclaimed himself to be the returned Hidden Imam, longed for by Shi'ites, and a prophet of God. His appearance is taken to imply the abrogation of Islam and the initiation of a new religious dispensation. After the Bab's death, Mirza Husayn 'Ali Nuri (1817–92), who took the name Baha'u'llah, proclaimed himself the messiah who had been promised by the Bab in the words 'He whom God shall make manifest'. Baha'u'llah's platform was strongly Modernist from the Muslim perspective within which it arose, and the Baha'i faith remains that way: legal reforms on matters such as women and family rights were implemented and disarmament, world government and inter-religious harmony became central proclamations, much in keeping with certain nineteenth-century European ideals (parallel to the Christian and Jewish case at the time).[14] From the perspective of the history of religions, this was an attempt to re-universalize Islam (even religion in general), taking it out of its culturally bound forms and into the modern context.

Like the Ahmadiyya, the Baha'is support a programme of modernization emerging from the context of Islam, but in this case not by a return to the sources and a renewal of the past; rather, this takes place by a replacement of the sources of authority (even though the Baha'is do revere the Qur'an, as they do all other scriptures, as the Word of God). This sort of radical rupture with the past is, of course, precisely what more conservative elements of society fear Modernists of all types are actually aiming towards.

The arguments for agnosticism and atheism present themselves as other possible solutions to the issues raised by modernity. The former, perhaps also to be seen as a simple embracing of secularism, is as rampant in many Muslim countries as it is elsewhere. Some may well argue that it is not really a solution as such; rather, it is a platform displaying a failure of nerve, the inability either to commit oneself to religion or to leave it totally. It is for many, however, a pragmatic solution where issues of religion are simply not as important in life as are matters of finding a job and maintaining a family.

Atheism is certainly present in the modern Muslim world, although many of those in the Middle East who have proclaimed it most loudly were Christians by family tradition rather than Muslims. Radical Marxism has been a powerful force in many Muslim countries, however, and it is in that context that one may best speak of an atheism. The denial of the theistic aspects of Islam entailed in this ideology places it outside the focus of interest for this discussion.

A MORE COMPLEX CATEGORIZATION

The preceding tri-partite division of Muslim movements – Traditionalist, Fundamentalist and Modernist – is functional in outlining major trends and attitudes but it does not sufficiently take into account the large number of in-between attitudes which are possible. A more complex but representative system is needed, although even then simplifications remain, especially when individuals are considered within a historical framework.

Recently, William Shepard published a thorough and significant article in which he argues for a five-part division of modern Muslim thought (with various subdivisions within several types) into secularism, Islamic modernism, radical Islamism, traditionalism and neo-traditionalism. The emphasis in Shepard's treatment, as indicated in the title of his paper, is on ideology; what is of concern, therefore, is the way in which world views orient an individual's actions towards social change. That is, these categories reflect, once again, the sense that what is being debated in Islam is not the religious fundamentals themselves, but the manner in which Islam should manifest itself as a social system. This focus on ideology should not, however, be allowed to obscure the religious elements lying beyond and behind these other aspects and should be kept in mind in all discussions.[15] Shepard's analysis may be summarized, as below, although this certainly excludes the many subtleties which he treats so astutely.[16]

Secularism, modernism, radical Islamism, traditionalism and neo-traditionalism

In looking at the first three of Shepard's divisions – secularism, modernism and radical Islamism – one factor differentiates or becomes crucial in the definition: the attitude towards what is termed 'Islamic totalism'. To what extent is Islam seen as encompassing all of life in its social, political and economic spheres? To what extent is Islam seen as a guide to social action and public legislation? The extent of this can range from Islam governing the full social structure to Islam being a 'religion' in a Protestant sense, that is, as a matter for the individual and his or her conscience alone. Here too, for Radical Islamists, as we shall see, it is possible to separate modernization and Westernization – that is, Islam can modernize without being Western, for Islam can be pictured as providing the basis for all of life and having nothing to do with the West, while at the same time change may be embraced as fully as is desired.

Islamic secularism

As was suggested above, secularization, as a process, is something which virtually everyone in the world confronts in one way or another. An embracing of the abstract ideal of secularism provides a definition applicable to this first category of Muslim approaches to the challenge of modernity: secularism will provide answers to the modern dilemmas, including those dilemmas perceived in secularization itself.

Secularism embraces those who argue for Islam in the modern world as a purely religious phenomenon without political force, so as to allow massive social reorganization. The extreme form of this is radical secularism as found in mid-twentieth-century Albania where the aim has been to replace all of Islam. It is, therefore, not Islamic as such, but since the people involved are Muslims by heritage and are seeking a way to live within the modern world, it can be meaningfully included in this category. More common is the type of secularism found in Turkey where there is a total separation of religion from politics and public life as a whole. Mustafa Kemal Atatürk (1881–1938) was the Turkish nationalist leader responsible for much of the character of that country as it is today. After leading the drive to expel the Greeks from Turkey after World War I, he moved the country towards official secularism, best typified symbolically by the change in the way Turkish was written: the Arabic script which had been used for five centuries under the Ottomans was abandoned and replaced by the Latin alphabet, modified slightly to account for certain particularities of Turkish. The suppression of Islamic legal and educational institutions and the outlawing of mystical Sufi groups were other steps in the removal of religion from the apparatus of the state. While certain elements of these positions have been modified in recent years, Turkey remains firmly Secularist. By way of an anecdote, it was reported that the lowering of the Turkish flag in front of government buildings on the occasion of Ayatullah Khumayni's death in 1989 caused quite a stir in the country, for it was felt that in doing this a foreign religious leader was being recognized by a self-proclaimed secular government.

Islam in officially secular countries is replaced, on an ideological level – that is, as the system of thought which orients and interprets an individual's life within society – by nationalism, capitalism or socialism. Other cited examples of secularism are termed by Shepard religious secularism (a multi-faith system), as in Indonesia, and Muslim secularism, as in Egypt during recent decades where religion (or Islam specifically) has a role and a standing politically but is not the full basis of the society. This can be seen in the way in which law codes have been implemented and adopted. While the Muslim religious legal code, the *shari'a*, has been replaced in secular countries by other law codes, in each instance the dividing line between religious and secular varies, especially when compared to Western models of secularism, as for example in the religious control of divorce and marriage. One other way in which secularism is characterized is by the state control of all religions. Secularism has been used to champion progress and also to enhance unity in countries, especially where there are significant non-Muslim minorities. This, it is said, has been the most important factor in pushing countries such as Egypt and Indonesia towards official secularism.

Islamic modernism

Islamic modernism wants Islam to be the basis for political life as well as the religious but perceives a need to reinterpret those structures in light of contemporary needs, frequently with clear and unapologetic adoption of Western notions. This generally reflects an idea of the flexibility of Islam, so that modern ideologies may be seen as fitting in with Islamic ones. Generally, Modernists (such as Fazlur Rahman and Ghulam Ahmad Parvez, to be discussed later in this book) argue that the juridical basis of Islam must be put aside for the modern use of independent judgement based on the Qur'an and *sunna*. This is a way of limiting the binding nature of the past, thus allowing some flexibility, but note that it does not deny the authority. Rather, it allows for a radical reinterpretation of the past, enabling the principles of the past to be seen in light of modern ideals, such as democracy, freedom, equality, tolerance and social justice. In fact, these and other ideals become general principles' which Islam is seen as standing for, and through which Islam must be implemented in today's world. Other examples are to be seen in the value of work, religious tolerance and the redistribution of excess wealth. Things which do not fit within these ideals are deemed superstitions and so to be done away with, for they are not in keeping with Islam. Notable too is the frequent Modernist appeal to the Islamic basis of many Western ideas – democracy being found in the early Islamic community, *dhimmi* (non-Muslim subjects living under Muslim rule) being religious pluralism, and so forth. This sort of tendency can lead to apologetics where the superiority of Islam over all things Western is argued, a tendency also to be seen, perhaps less frequently, in radical Islamism. (As Shepard says,[17] this claim is not necessarily wrong, but it does leave the question, 'so what?') Modernism, then, differs from secularism in the efforts it makes to find support in the Qur'an and the *sunna*; from the critic's point of view, this method is only 'a cover for what secularists do more openly'.[18]

Radical Islamism

Radical Islamism is what is also called 'fundamentalism', a term borrowed from early twentieth-century Christianity to which Shepard has devoted another article.[19] As a term applied to Islam, fundamentalism raises various problems which need to be confronted. In its application to religious groupings, the word 'fundamentalism' arose in the United States and was used by a coalition of theologically conservative Protestants who came together in 1920 to struggle against modernism and liberalism; it was coined because these people were said to be holding to the great fundamentals of their faith.[20] For Protestant Fundamentalists, the key fundamental is the inerrancy of the Bible, a stance which is a defence of basic religious ideals – the seriousness of sin, the need for redemption and the idea that Jesus has granted that redemption. There is a great stress placed on individual salvation and personal morality. Fundamentalists are prepared to do battle for their fundamentals. The best examples are seen in court cases against the teaching of evolution in the 1920s and in the more contemporary 'moral majority' movement.

In the Islamic world the term fundamentalism has been applied (mainly by Westerners) to those who call for a strict implementation of the *shari'a*, including the call for an Islamic state. Opposition to Western ways and to the perceived corruption of society is important, and even, according to some,[21] the most important element uniting Fundamentalists of all religious persuasions.

The issue of scripture marks a difference between Muslim and Christian Fundamentalists. Virtually all Muslims are 'fundamentalist' in their attitude to scripture. And, on the other hand, the Protestant doctrines which are seen as intimately linked to inerrancy (for example, the resurrection of Jesus) are rejected by all Muslims. Likewise, while Muslim Fundamentalists stress political goals and implementation of religion in all areas of life, Christian Fundamentalists can go either way, and some become Secularists by Muslim standards.

One point in this regard is worth repeating. Fundamentalism in the Islamic world is often seen to have started with the Wahhabis in eighteenth-century Arabia, as was mentioned above. This was very much an internal Islamic movement and not at all a reaction to the concept of modernity as that term has been defined here.[22] The difference, however, depends on precisely how one defines fundamentalism in the Islamic sphere; the Wahhabis may well be termed, in Shepard's categories, neo-Traditionalists.

Similarities

The oppositional stance of both Christian and Muslim Fundamentalist groups is significant; they both 'do battle' with Western modernism. (Muslims also frequently attack elements within their own societies and desire a total restructuring.) That element of militancy on behalf of God's way in the world unites both groups. The claim to be the authentic expression of the tradition is also prominent; ironically, then, both groups – Christians and Muslims – emphasize the distinctive elements of their own faith. Both groups wish to take scripture very seriously (if not always literally, although in theory they may be more inclined that way than more Modernist groups). Absolutism in ethics follows from this and both groups emphasize the supernatural, seeing God's will at work in the world in very direct ways.

Islamic fundamentalism – radical Islamism

Certainly Islam is all-encompassing for the Fundamentalists such as Abul A'la Mawdudi and Sayyid Qutb, as it is for the Modernists, but the emphasis is far more on the legitimacy of past solutions to modern problems. Islam is unique and distinctive in the view of radical Islamism, and comparisons of Islam to the West, as made by many Modernists, are false. This is not a rejection of the West as such, however, for these people are generally ready to adopt modern technology and political organization. An example of this attitude is that the Islamic principle of *dhimma* (traditionally a word referring to Jews and Christians who live within the Islamic world and are granted the status of protected communities) should be upheld for what it is and not the Western principle of equality before the law. This is often spoken of in terms of Islamic authenticity, which becomes an anti-apologetic stance; it is not necessary to explain Islam in terms of Western ideals, as the apologists for Islam do (especially the early Modernists), for all can be expressed through reference to an Islamic bedrock.

Islam is the basis for all life, is flexible, non-superstitious and encourages independent reasoning (*ijtihad*), all those factors being held in common with modernism. Constraints are seen on *ijtihad*: this must be practised in a truly Islamic way on the basis of clear texts and only where those texts clearly need elaboration. Progress through Islam and not turning the clock back to the untarnished past is crucial; what is needed in order to accomplish this is the implementation of the Islamic *shari'a*. The main difference between the Radical Islamists and the Modernists is the degree to which Islam is seen as governing all of life. For the Radical Islamists, modernity may be embraced, but not to the extent of modifying what are argued to be essential elements of the faith – Sunday for *juma'* prayer, rather than Friday, since it is more convenient, or the abolition of Ramadan for purposes of increasing production are to be rejected. Another point which distinguishes the groups is the Fundamentalist argument that the Qur'anic society is by no means an unobtainable ideal: it is very practical, within reach and worth pursuing; Modernists tend to see the ideal as one towards which Muslims must keep striving ceaselessly.

Revolutionary radical Islamism – that fringe element which dominates the media picture of Islamic fundamentalism – is distinct in the emphasis it places on the corruption of Islam from within the community. True Islam is the cure and must be applied through armed uprising. Also notable is the tendency to view things as opposing spheres: for example, the government of God versus the Great Satan in Iranian propaganda. Thus for someone such as Sayyid Qutb everything is *jahili*, from the 'age of barbarism', except Islam.

Islamic traditionalism

Traditionalism maintains its allegiance to past methods and has not dealt with the threat and the attraction of the West; such views are found, according to Shepard, among the elite, Sufis and the lower classes, and in the Saudi Arabian context. Westernization is a temptation from God, to be resisted. There are, however, two major tendencies within the Traditionalists: the Rejectionists, who argue for the outright rejection of the West, and the Adaptationists, who use delaying techniques in order to stall the change which may be seen as inevitable. Certainly change is experienced by all these groups but the time-honoured ways of dealing with it are deemed sufficient.

Neo-traditionalism

Neo-traditionalism is seen as a transitional position from traditionalism to any of the other groups. It may be, however, that as a position it has its own inherent permanent protagonists; such a position (displayed in S.H. Nasr's writings and, perhaps, in the Iranian revolution)[23] urges a gradual change, seeing the advantage in certain elements of modern technology, for example, but wanting to withstand the rush of the acceptance of it all. In the short term, urgent change may be required but, in the long run, Islam will reign supreme. Here, too, we encounter Rejectionists, who wish to use an Islamic basis for changing the status quo of society, and Adaptationists, who encourage the use of more modern techniques.

MUSLIM INTELLECTUALISM: YET ANOTHER CATEGORY?

But in all these sorts of analysis – whether they be tri-partite or penta-partite, whether applied to Judaism, Christianity or Islam, and despite any lingering debate over the accuracy of the terminology and description – there would seem to be a prominent section of modern ideology missing. What to term this is difficult, but 'intellectualist' might work. It would not seem possible to study modern Christianity without taking into account Hans Küng, for example, nor could we consider modern Judaism without Emil Fackenheim. Neither of these people can claim a very substantial portion of the believers within the religion as his followers, it might be argued, yet it would seem that a picture of those religions within the modern world would be incomplete without them.

In fact, in the cases of Judaism and Christianity, I do not perceive that there is much difficulty in including such figures in a survey of modern thought; it is more likely that the more conservative sides of those two religions are going to be dismissed as having no significantly enunciated platform to be discussed. When we come to the study of modern Islam, however, the case seems to be different. Attention to the intellectual side seems to be sadly lacking. Many reasons for this can be suggested. Often the excuse is made that the intellectual trend does not seem significant numerically within Islam (especially as compared to modern Judaism and Christianity). Where are we supposed to turn to find the impact of such people? Yet it would seem like a not-too-paranoid reaction to suggest, in this era of the ramifications of attacks on Orientalism by people such as Edward Said,[24] that the suspicion is that this ignoring of the intellectual trend is a part of the necessary degradation of Islam itself by Orientalists. To credit Islam with the possibility of such persons existing would seem to be counter to the basic Orientalist stance of picturing Islam as a constraining and reactionary force.[25]

As discussed at the end of Part I of this book, Mohammed Arkoun is one of those intellectuals who is often ignored, not being considered representative of anything to do with modern Islam itself. The first impression some people receive of a figure such as Arkoun is one of a person who has 'sold out' to the West, a person who has adopted so much of the European intellectual tradition that there is no Islamic root left in any meaningful way. Of course, it is a fact that, in general, many of the intellectuals found in modern religions do live and work in the university context and conduct themselves as academics with all that requires – learned papers, prolific production of books and articles – and this seems to give some credence to the stance that such people do not need to be considered part of the intellectual construct of the given religion as such. This may account for some of the reality behind the idea that there do not seem to be many people like Arkoun in Islam: many perhaps are lurking within our universities without ever identifying themselves in a particularly overt way.

Arkoun himself wants to use the term 'the critical tendency in current Islamic thought' when speaking of the 'intellectual and scientific directions' in modern Muslim thinking. Significantly, in terms of understanding how his position fits into the overall picture, he has clearly attempted to embrace what he would term a *contemporary* theoretical stance (as opposed to simply modern, that being equated to a historicist perspective), and this he sees as the basis of his work.

Mohammed Arkoun passionately believes that what he has to say is of relevance not only to the university academic tradition but also to the Muslim faith. The claim is that what he says should have some bearing on the basic understanding of faith in the modern world and on how that faith should be expressed and understood, not only in the academic framework but also from within the faith's perspective. His position may represent a thread of Islamic modernism in the intellectual, theological sense, but it is one which is very attuned to the close of the twentieth century and thus, as was suggested earlier, post-Modernist may be a better term. Other Modernists, from a lay background (as is apparently the case with Arkoun), have pursued scholarship but have frequently found theological liberalism too dangerous a course to follow. Whether that will change in the future we must wait and see.

ANOTHER NEW TENDENCY

The claim has been made above – and the very categories suggested for the analysis only act to confirm that claim – that it is the ideological aspects of Islam that are at issue; theological reflection, in the way that term would be traditionally understood (and thus excluding Arkoun, whose approach embraces all such aspects as well), seems to be absent.

A startling exception is the recent book by Shabbir Akhtar.[26] Akhtar became famous during the uproar over Salman Rushdie's *The Satanic Verses*; he became an extremely eloquent spokesman for the Muslim community, especially in Bradford, England, where much of the controversy centred. Akhtar has a Doctorate in Philosophy of Religion and brings to the modern expression of Islam precisely that which is said to be missing: a theological re-evaluation of Islam, expressed in modern philosophical terms. Consider the following:

> The silence of God in this increasingly religionless age is certainly damaging to the faithful outlook. It does seem to open up the possibility of supplying impressively plausible cases for the atheistic stance. Indeed it creates a serious doubt about God's alleged miraculous activities even in the past. Is it not an arguably superior assumption that the different human claims about the miraculous are better explicable in terms of a cultural shift in our thinking rather than in terms of God's decision to introduce in recent years a basic alteration in his ways? Given the credulity and gullibility of early man, his ignorance of the moods of Nature – an ignorance poorly compensated by the pagan appeal to magic and its illusory technique – the atheist's suggestion is surely not altogether implausible.
>
>   The current silence of Allah could spell a crisis for Muslim faith. Nature is as revealing as it is ambiguous, hence of course the need for a

revelation in a sacred language in the first place. The God of Islam seems to have retreated from Nature and community, the two matrices in which, according to religious believers, he typically used to reveal himself.[27]

Akhtar's point is that the challenges of contemporary philosophy to the tenability of religious faith as a whole have been ignored by Muslims but can only continue to be ignored at the peril of the survival of the faith itself. Christianity, for Akhtar, has virtually self-destructed through the efforts of (Protestant) theologians bending over backwards to assimilate the latest theories of secularism to their faith. This will happen to Islam too if the example of Christianity is not studied carefully nor lessons learned from the mistakes made in that arena.

Akhtar's theological position tends to support the traditional side of radical Islamism. Most significant is the aspect of the all-encompassing nature of Islam (Christianity's 'render unto Caesar what is Caesar's' has, it would appear for Akhtar, been misused in recent centuries to support separation of church and state). But it is in the reformulation of philo-sophically supported arguments in favour of traditional Islamic doctrine – the inerrancy of the Qur'an,[28] the eternal message of scripture, the concept of the one God – where Akhtar, as he says of himself, breaks new ground. Just what the future might hold for this development is certainly unclear. For many Muslims, it would seem that even the opening of such questions for debate is going too far. For Akhtar, however, the failure to treat such questions openly and honestly could spell the end of Islam as a viable religion in the modern, secular context. Akhtar's inquiries are likely to move him out of the Fundamentalist camp which, at this point, he defends 'out of a desire to empathise with members of his own community, to avoid taking the road that enticed the intellectually gifted sons of Islam into the enemy camp, so to speak'.[29] In other words, Akhtar has not yet created for himself (and those like him) a philosophically integrated and consistent stance within Islam; further work in the area and, as Malise Ruthven has pointed out, greater exposure to the classics of Muslim philosophy, theology and history may well yet produce that new vision.

Part III

Muhammad: his life and his authority

3 Muhammad and his biographers

THE *SUNNA* AND ITS AUTHORITY

It was suggested in the previous part of this volume that it is crucial to any understanding of religion in the modern world that an assessment of the attitude towards the past be undertaken: how is the authority of the past dealt with in the modern situation? In the Islamic case, the many specific issues which arise stem from one major question: what is the status of Muhammad and the Qur'an in the view of modern Muslims?

In dealing with Muhammad, there are a number of approaches that may be contemplated in order to embrace the totality of the subject. Muhammad's role as a source of authority through the status of what he actually did during his lifetime, summed up in the word *sunna*, is crucial. This will be dealt with in the next chapter. There are other, more subtle ways in which Muhammad is discussed in the modern context, however, each of which reflects the impact of modernity and differing conceptions of Islam. They are frequently implicit positions, versus the explicit ones found in the discussions of the *sunna* and its authority. They are often more popular and significant in terms of their influence.

All Muslim groups in the modern world join in their veneration of Muhammad. In fact, within the context of the modern world, that must be taken as one of the defining elements of what Islam actually is. The writing of biographies of Muhammad is, therefore, a singularly appropriate enterprise for all concerned and is one to which we should now turn our attention.

THE ROLE OF BIOGRAPHY

Biographies of Muhammad allow one to gain some initial insight into the modern Muslim notion of the prophet. Biography is a powerful mirror for the reflection of the ideals, as well as the standards, of the age in which it is written, and thus may be seen to reflect the contemporary situation of its authors in the very construction of the facts which the work intends to record.

Because of Muhammad's role in Islamic society as 'teacher and exemplar'[1] – ideals embodied in the concept of the *sunna* – his life story has been used constantly as an inspirational source, manifesting itself in the writing of biographies. With the impact of change in the modern world, it has become necessary for a biographer to create a biography which may be read as having some relevance to the modern world: a relevance which will reflect the ideals and aspirations of the writer's perception of the needs of the Muslim community. For example, encouraging the use of reason, the pursuit of education and the fostering of science have frequently been pictured as cures for the ills of the Muslim world. Providing women with a more active role in society has become another common goal. The support that the actual details of the life of Muhammad can provide to these ideas is crucial to the process of legitimizing the change which is deemed necessary. The sense of legitimization is important for most reformers; if Islam is to remain relevant to human life, then the changes deemed desirable must be incorporated within it. There is also a pragmatic reason for the appeal to legitimization by Muhammad: literature, especially of the biographical type, is a powerful tool of propaganda.

Furthermore, biographies can become a vehicle for reformers, as a message couched in traditional terms and thus not so subject to attack from the more conservative elements in society. The example of widely criticized reformers from the nineteenth century made a number of their twentieth-century counterparts feel the need to veil their ideas in a form acceptable (or less easy to reject out-of-hand) to the religious powers.

The character of biography

A number of motifs are found repeatedly in modern biographies of Muhammad which are worthy of attention. Among these are the following:

1 The treatment of the process of revelation versus the role of reason – can the traditional view of revelation as a supernatural event be maintained in the light of reason?

2 The issue of Muhammad's sinlessness – does it really make sense that Muhammad never committed an error during his life as has been traditionally held?

3 The nature of Muhammad's heavenly journey, undertaken early in his prophetic career, according to traditional accounts, when he travelled on the back of a winged horse to Jerusalem and ascended to heaven in order to meet the former prophets and receive a vision of God – was it in the

body (as was classically emphasized) or by the soul only (perhaps as a vision)?[2]

4 The general status of miracles in Muhammad's life – can they be accounted for by rational scientific explanations?

5 Muhammad's personality as a husband and as a statesman, with *jihad*, 'holy war', a major part of the issue – can these sorts of activity be accepted in a modern context?

These topics reflect two concerns, both prominently displayed in the biographies. One is the impact of modern scientific thought and ways of understanding phenomena such as prophecy and miraculous occurrences. The other is the impact of Orientalism and general Christian attacks on Islam, especially in charges of Muhammad's 'immorality' (as reflected, for example, in concerns over the number of his marriages) and 'war-mongering' (as reflected in the assessment of the many battles which he led against the various tribes in Arabia). This last point is somewhat more complex. Orientalists, especially those who worked within the framework of colonialist regimes, frequently accused Islam of being counter to modern ideals and progress, that concept being glossed to include morality and ethics. That is, the morality encouraged by Islam was not in keeping with the modern ethos and would only hold Muslims back from being able to embrace science and progress. An example would be the horror expressed by some writers at the idea of Muslim men being able to have four wives; no man could possibly be an active member of an industrialized work force and cope with four wives! Therefore, these two topics – modern scientific thought and the moral character of Islam – are frequently intertwined. The pro-science argument is anti-Orientalist at the same time.

With regard to the Orientalist attention to Muhammad, while Muslim devotion to their prophet was obvious enough, Christian desires to discover the 'historical Jesus' were undoubtedly reflected in some of the attention being given to Muhammad. The temptation towards implicit or explicit comparisons between Jesus and Muhammad – always being conducted from the viewpoint of the superiority of Christianity, to be sure – was undoubtedly too hard to resist for many Orientalist writers.

The question of the historical reliability of sources and the rise of historical criticism has also affected the Muslim biographical enterprise to a great extent. In embracing ideals of modern scientific thought and in rejecting Orientalist aspersions on Islam, a method of historical-critical writing arose. This rise of the study of history is one of the characteristics of the modern period, as was suggested in Part I of this volume. There was, therefore, on the part of some modern Muslim writers, an effort to foster a historical-critical approach in their writings about Muhammad. No longer, it was said, could events simply be narrated as they were in the past, but the sources must be subjected to analysis for bias and implausibility. For those reformers bent on introducing the scientific method into the Muslim world, what more appropriate (but potentially dangerous!) vehicle could there be than the biography of Muhammad? Many writers therefore certainly raise these sorts of issue in their work, but, in many instances, the actual implementation of the historical method has been quite minimal. That fact, however, should not detract from the attention given to the influence the idea itself has had.

Biographies and history

The emphasis in many (but certainly not all) of the modern biographies is not on Muhammad's actions as such – that is, not as in the historical narratives found in the classical books written by people like Ibn Ishaq (d. 767) – but on his spiritual attitude, his general outlook and his morals. In this sense, Muhammad is portrayed as the truly modern man and, once that idea is fully understood, then Islam may not only be seen to be compatible with the modern era but may also be seen to embody it fully.

In Volume 1 of this work, I wrote that the classical biography of Muhammad was a mythic portrayal of a pristine society at the time of the foundation of Islam: it depicts the Islamic ideal. The classical biographies are then no different from the modern ones in their intentions. Each wishes to portray the ideals of the community, but the fact is that those ideals have changed over time. For the classical biographer Ibn Ishaq, valiant battles led by the divinely appointed leader of the community served as an example for all to follow. Muhammad's special relationship to God was displayed by the permission granted to him to marry many wives. These were aspects of the argument for Islam at the time of Ibn Ishaq. But for modern writers, the ideals and aspirations are different and narrating the factual realities of Muhammad's life (as recorded in these classical sources) does not necessarily accomplish the desired goal of contemporary relevance. In fact, Muhammad as a real, live person tends to fade in many of the modern biographies, slipping into the light of unreal, absolute perfection in his heroic role, while at the same time there is a downplaying of the 'irrational' prophetic elements in his life. Muhammad's greatest miracle for many modern writers, unlike the ancient writers such as Ibn Ishaq, is not the splitting of the moon, or the sighing palm trunk as he walked by, or talking sheep, but the moral and spiritual transformation which he accomplished in society.

Another aspect appears in some biographies which needs attention: the biographies frequently reflect the socio-political environment of the writer to the extent that support for specific political parties becomes manifest. The past becomes a source of inspiration, especially for nationalists, and nationalism was rife in Egypt in the 1930s, for example, reflecting internal developments but also trends in European political thought; Islam and Muhammad became ideal channels through which nationalism could be expressed. There was a wave of biographical writing in Egypt during this period; as a result, treatments of Muhammad became popular elsewhere in the Arab world, the biographical form being adopted as a vehicle for reform. Looking at a number of these biographies briefly will indicate some of their scope. Most of the attention falls on Muhammad Husayn Haykal, the most significant and the most studied of all contemporary biographers.[3]

MUHAMMAD HUSAYN HAYKAL

Muhammad Haykal was born in 1888 and died in 1956. He studied law in Cairo and then pursued further education at the Sorbonne in Paris. He received his Doctorate in 1912 for studies in economics and law. He worked as a lawyer and educator, as a member of the government, as a novelist and, most significantly, as a journalist. His first work, *Zaynab*, was written while he was in Paris and was published in 1914; it is generally cited as the first Arabic novel. He also founded a newspaper with a weekly literary supplement in the 1920s and much of his later work appeared in it.

Haykal's Islam

Haykal is most concerned with establishing the rationality of Islam and rejecting every Orientalist objection to, and criticism of, the religion itself. Islam is, for Haykal, fully in keeping with modern life and reason. Modern rational standards may, in fact, be identified as inherently and originally Muslim, Greek and Egyptian. Writes Haykal,

> Long before the times of Moses and Jesus, the science of ancient Egypt as well as its philosophy and law had passed to Greece and Rome, which had then spread their dominion. It was Egypt that contributed to Greek philosophy and literature their noblest ideas. The new rationalist awakening thus produced, warned and convinced people that miracles constitute no argument at all ... it was God's pattern that reason shall constitute the apogee of human life, as long as it is not composed of empty logic, not devoid of feeling and spirit, and as long as it martials all these faculties in a synthesized effort to discover the secrets of the universe and achieve intimate knowledge of the cosmic pattern. Thus, it was decreed by God that soon the Prophet of Islam would rise to call men to the truth through reason, complemented by feeling and spirit, and that the one

miracle of such a gnoseological synthesis should be the Holy Book revealed to his Prophet Muhammad.[4]

Much of this paragraph is a reaction against Christian missionary and Orientalist prejudice and is spoken of as a scientific inquiry into Muhammad, away from the biases of the Europeans. Haykal does use European studies of Muhammad as the basis of his work, however, for he considered the traditional Arabic sources to be full of superstition and impossible stories. To some extent, Haykal suggests, the Orientalists are not to blame for their distortions of Islam, for irrational elements are clearly to be found in the classical sources. It should not be thought, however, that Haykal simply employs the historical-critical method as expounded in the West; rather his biography of Muhammad is guided by the ideals and spirit of Islam and by the sources moulded by the methodological principle that things 'must have been' a certain way. It is generally not a critical analysis entailing a comparison of various traditions, but simply a choosing of the appropriate historical report through the elimination of any elements deemed superstitious or in error according to the modern sensibility.

Notably, Haykal also sees his approach as a rejection of Muslim conservative elements. What is holding Muslims back is not Islam but the tradition which is so fervently maintained by the religious elite. Furthermore, the attitudes displayed by the conservative religious authorities only give the Orientalists and the Christian missionaries more ammunition. The sources used by these unfriendly writers are those dominated by the conservative elements, and the conclusions which those people come to are the result not of the methodology which they employ – a methodology which Haykal argues should be followed – but of the sources themselves.

The only absolutely reliable source for talking about Islam is the Qur'an. Interpreting the other sources in the light of the spirit of the Qur'an would correct all misunderstandings. Clearly, for Haykal, the message of the Qur'an is one of rationality and the search for scientific wisdom, and that is a message which the religious classes have perverted over the ages. Further, the Qur'an supports ideas of social order and individual freedom, keys to a truly modern Islamic society and in agreement with Haykal's own political position.[5]

Haykal's Muhammad

Haykal's work, *The Life of Muhammad*, published as a book in 1935, has been extensively read, translated and studied, in a popular way as well as in scholarly analyses. Its aim is to provide a fully modern biography, one written in accord with modern scientific reason. At the same time, it is not a critical biography: for the most part it is a reiteration of facts from the classical sources with no critical stance. Haykal started the work in 1932 and published pieces of it periodically over the following two years. The work has been through at least ten editions, gaining a few extra sections in the process.

Haykal argues that all biographers reflect the standards of their own day. That Ibn Ishaq, for example, should speak of certain events as miraculous simply reflects his understanding of the workings of the world at his time. Likewise, the early biographers display a materialistic slant towards an issue such as Muhammad's multiple marriages (emphasizing elements like tribal alliances and so forth) and fail to see the spiritual element implied by the prophet's activities.

Several points prove crucial in Haykal's biography, as they do in most modern biographies, for they reflect the central issues which have been emphasized in Western attacks upon Muhammad and Islam: this apologetic response of the biographers is frequently their most notable element. Haykal discusses the trustworthiness of Muhammad to counter some of the charges laid against him. Involved here is the notion of Muhammad's sinlessness. One special aspect of this regards the 'Satanic verses', concerning which it is declared inconceivable that Muhammad could have been deceived by Satan into uttering certain verses supposedly in the Qur'an (but later withdrawn) which compromised the monotheism of Islam by allowing minor goddesses to be viewed as intercessors with Allah (a story told in many classical sources). Muhammad's marriages are dealt with in detail, especially those to Zaynab and Mariya where images of lust and seduction were often conjured up. The treatment of Muhammad's use of violence, minimized as much as possible by Haykal, is especially noticeable in comparison with older texts, where Muhammad's fighting is often seen as a part of his successful strategy and nothing to be played down: fighting took place under God's will and command. All these areas are focused upon by Orientalists, and Haykal clearly rejects the Orientalist conclusions and the process by which they arrived at them.

Finally, Haykal speaks from a certain time period in Egypt when democracy was being promoted; his biography clearly reflects those ideals as stemming from, and therefore legitimized by, the time of Muhammad.

While the non-Muslim inhabitants began to fear Muslim power – knowing well that it stemmed from the depth of hearts which had tasted sacrifice and persecution for the sake of faith, the Muslims collected the fruits of their patience and enjoyed their religious freedom. Their peace and freedom were now made constitutional by the Islamic principles that no man has any authority over any other, that religion belongs to God alone, that service is to Him alone, that before Him all men are absolutely equal, and that nothing differentiates them except their works and intentions. . . . The theater was ready and the stage was set for Muhammad to constitute by his conduct the ideal exemplification and embodiment of these teachings and principles, and for his laying down the foundation stone of Islamic civilization.[6]

Because of Haykal's sense of rationality, he sees fewer miracles playing a role in Muhammad's life but puts an emphasis on natural processes to explain some of them. The heavenly journey is taken as psychological, for example. As well, the picture of Muhammad is framed in terms of modern ideals – loving, forgiving, perfect.

TAHA HUSAYN

Taha Husayn (1889–1973), an Egyptian novelist and educator, published three volumes in 1933, 1937 and 1946 called *On the Margin of the Biography of Muhammad*. Born in rural Egypt, educated in traditional Qur'anic schools and blind from a very young age, Taha Husayn represents, for much of the early twentieth-century Arab world, the movement from a medieval to a modern world view. After undergoing a religious education, including a period studying at al-Azhar, the bastion of Islamic orthodoxy even today, Taha Husayn studied at the Egyptian University of Cairo and received a PhD for his work on the Arab poet al-Ma'arri. He then went to the Sorbonne in Paris and received another degree for his study of the historian/sociologist Ibn Khaldun. He became Minister of Education in Egypt and wrote novels, an autobiography and many works of scholarship, all reflecting a profound respect for tradition while embracing contemporary ideals and scholarly processes. He became embroiled in controversy over a work of his which expressed doubts about the genuineness of the preserved portions of pre-Islamic poetry, the study being seen by traditional religious scholars as an attack on the foundations of Islam. The method which he used in this investigation, as in his other works, is summarized by him in the following words: 'It is my desire that we should not accept anything of what the ancients said about our literature and its history, except after examination and confirmation.' This method is 'the course followed by modern scientists and philosophers in their treatment of science and philosophy. I propose to apply to literature the philosophical method originated by Descartes.'[7]

Taha Husayn's emphasis while writing about Muhammad was always on the cultural heritage which was to be found in classical works such as the *Sira* of Ibn Ishaq. Such writings are a source of pride and are of relevance to modern Muslims precisely because of their ability to inspire the reader. This was, in fact, true of all the great works of the Arab past, which represents 'one of the high points of an ongoing Western civilization'[8] according to Taha Husayn's general philosophy of history. This respect for, and revival of, the heritage of Arab civilization would provide the vehicle for the construction of a new Egypt.

The retelling of the story of Muhammad, then, was done in an imaginative way, recounting events from the perspective of various characters living at the time of Muhammad and presented in a rational fashion without any emphasis on miraculous actions or the like. However, the element of the fulfilment of people's expectations of a prophet, the 'bearer of truth, light and reason',[9] is played up to the fullest extent. In matters of the role of reason, Taha Husayn simply denies that Muhammad performed any miracles.

'ABBAS MAHMUD AL-'AQQAD

Al-'Aqqad (1889–1964) published *The Genius of Muhammad* in 1942. Responding to the popularity of Thomas Carlyle's essay, 'The Hero as Prophet', and seeing the need to produce an insider's appreciation of Muhammad, this biography too is marked by its tendency to react to European impressions of Muhammad. Muhammad is the great prophet, the great hero, the great man for all Muslims; his political life is therefore not as important as his spiritual one. As a result, al-'Aqqad's biography downplays events as such and concentrates on the character of the hero. Muhammad was sent to a decaying world, one which lacked belief and order, so his role was one of a prophet, combining the functions of preacher, military leader, statesman and organizer. His was a message based on love and his heroism did not stem from the sword; rather, his wars were defensive and his marriages brought enhanced status to the women involved and to the community in general. Furthermore, Muhammad's message and life proved his superiority to all other persons on the stage of world history. Muhammad's military prowess was superior even to that displayed by Napoleon and Hitler, according to al-'Aqqad.[10] That the world today once again needs to appreciate the message of Muhammad in order to solve its problems is implicit in al-'Aqqad's presentation.

'ABD AL-RAHMAN AL-SHARQAWI

Al-Sharqawi (1920–87) was an Egyptian novelist and critic who, in 1962, published *Muhammad, the Messenger of Freedom*. His previous writings were famous for their poetic spirit as well as their political commitment. His treatment of Muhammad was not designed as a biography to replace the classical ones in their recounting of history; 'everything has been said' on that topic, according to the author. Rather, he was attempting to portray an image of Muhammad as a man whose aim was to produce a unified humanity based on notions of love and mercy and whose ultimate goal was to produce a better future for his people. Inherent in Muhammad's message was progress and liberation through a veritable revolution.[11]

Al-Sharqawi hoped to provide a positive picture for non-Muslim readers, a potentially large and fruitful audience given the sizeable population of Christian Copts in Egypt. His work also, and perhaps more successfully, reflects the political climate of Nasserite socialism in Egypt, a revolt against capitalism (and thus against Europe). This is conveyed by picturing Muhammad as a worker, rising up on behalf of others against the rich Quraysh tribe and the Jews; the latter are pictured throughout the work as the rich enemies whom Muhammad constantly tried to befriend. Downplayed are the prophetic and miraculous elements in Muhammad's life; his experiences are seen as dreams of the perfect state of human existence, free from the type of oppression which was prevalent in pre-Islamic Mecca where everything was done for the benefit of the rich. Al-Sharqawi's biography, then, is apologetic while pursuing the clear political end of a modern vision of society legitimized through Muhammad's life. As such, it aroused some opposition within Egyptian clerical circles for its failure to treat the traditional religious values of Muhammad's career and Islam as a whole.

'ABD AL-RAHMAN 'AZZAM

'Azzam (1893–1976) was an Egyptian diplomat and served as Secretary-General of the Arab League from 1945 to 1952. In 1938 he wrote an Arabic work entitled *The Hero of Heroes or the most Prominent Attribute of the Prophet Muhammad*. A revised English version was published in 1965 as *The Eternal Message of Muhammad*. The format of the book is worthy of attention. The life of Muhammad itself is briefly sketched in a short twenty pages. Following that are sections dealing with the basic message of Islam, social reform, the state, international relations, dissemination of the message, the causes of world disturbances, and the search for 'a spiritual bulwark for civilization'. The point is clear: Muhammad, through his person and his action, has something to say about each of these aspects of modern (political) existence. Bravery, love, the ability to forgive, and eloquence are all attributes of Muhammad that are emphasized, leading to the conclusion that the diplomatic nature of Muhammad's life is one that provides an example for today in the resolution of conflicts.

The Message of Muhammad recognizes neither nationalism nor racism in their modern contexts; the fatherland of the Muslim admits of no geographical delimitations – it coexists with the faith. . . . Racism, or a fanatic attachment to tribe, nation, color, language, or culture, is rejected by the Message as a product of pre-Islamic idolatry.[12]

Political manoeuvres and military insights are also claimed:

> Recognizing the inherent and manifest evils of war, the Message of Muhammad circumscribed warfare with common rules of right conduct (*adab*), defining its aims and limiting it to the repulsion of aggression, the protection of the freedom of belief, and the termination of battle with just and durable agreements. . . . Certain states nowadays prefer surprise attacks on their enemies without any previous warning. Preliminary precautions prior to attack are such that the aggression-bent state can surprise its enemies completely by pretending all along to favor peace; often the true motives and pretenses for waging war may not be revealed prior to combat. . . . There is nothing more distasteful to Islam than this, and the tenets of Muslim law reject it in spirit and in practice.[13]

TRENDS IN MORE RECENT BIOGRAPHIES

The second half of the twentieth century has seen the figure of Muhammad used in a wide variety of ways in modern Muslim countries. There has been the film *The Messenger*, although the person of Muhammad himself was never portrayed. Novels have appeared, employing him as a character. The biographical form has become looser and the treatments' tendencies towards stating certain positions are more marked. These modifications may well reflect the increasing disparity between the Modernists and the Fundamentalists in more recent decades, all of whom continue to appeal to the biography of Muhammad to support their positions. Of course, alongside these radical trends, the more traditional production of biographies has continued, still influenced by ideas of modern rationality and science, but displaying very little difference from earlier attempts.[14]

NAGUIB MAHFOUZ

Awarded the Nobel Prize for Literature in 1988, Mahfouz is probably the best known of all contemporary Arab writers. Born in 1911, he published his first novel in 1939 at a time when the Arabic novel as a form was in its infancy. His major works include *The Cairene Trilogy*, written 1956–7, which traces the story of three generations of a Cairo family, putting into novel form the changes in the daily life of middle-class people in the first half of the twentieth century. His works were cited by the Nobel Prize committee as being 'rich in nuance, now clearsightedly realistic, now evocatively ambiguous'.

Mahfouz's vision of Islam

Mahfouz, in at least some of his writings, critiques the stance and values of traditional religion, Islam included. Religion has not accomplished what it set out to do. The Divine has become irrelevant to modern life because of the way in which he has been made absent from human existence. The prophets, sent by God, have had little effect on human existence, 'unable after their demise to ensure any abiding salvation for mankind from the burden of being human'.[15]

Mahfouz's Muhammad

Published first as a serial in the newspaper *al-Ahram* in 1959, *Children of Gabalawi* is an allegory of God, his messengers through history and their interaction with the world. Its treatment of Muhammad is not therefore traditional biography by any means, although elements of his life as depicted in early works are clearly discernible in the character of Qasim and his environs of the streets of Cairo. The names are changed 'to protect the innocent', but the story remains the same. The book is even divided into 114 sections, echoing the 114 *sura*s of the Qur'an.

Mahfouz's Muhammad is a deeply committed man who challenges the established secular and religious powers. He leads a band of vigilantes whose aim is no less than setting the stage for a world where human rights are respected and the law of God is enacted; this they set out to accomplish by force, in a manner pictured as being midway between Moses' war-mongering and Jesus' pacifism. Muhammad's character embodies all the values that should be emulated and this includes his ability to love women; no modern apologetic is needed to excuse Muhammad's multiple marriages.[16]

Mahfouz's main interest, however, is in the frustration of the goal of Muhammad by later followers, and this is what the work goes on to explore in its final section. Science has become the prophet. The leaders of the past have been made into legends. The story finally leads to the death of Gabalawi (i.e. God). Muhammad, in this way, is no different from the earlier prophets talked of in the book (Adam, Moses, Jesus) whose mission should have been sufficient to set the world aright, but, in fact, matters did not work out that way. Muslims are now without God, even while they claim to be surrounded by him; this is the result of the failure to pose the necessary and penetrating questions concerning the nature of God and existence.

This is a biography for the modern world, one in which the message is deeply veiled by the curtain of the medium and the form. One cannot help thinking of Salman Rushdie's attempt at the same feat, and this parallel has been pursued by some observers.[17] Mahfouz's work created an outcry at the time of its publication and it did not appear in book form until it was published in Beirut (the venue for many a dissident Egyptian work) in 1967. Kenneth Cragg's assessment of the work is fitting:

> Its haunting, wistful scepticism presents a searching challenge to ordinary believers. Served by eminent narrative skill and literary art, it invites them to look into a void, to think themselves stripped of their familiar securities, to divest themselves of assumptions about God and His messengers which have always been instinctive to their minds and culture. It confronts them with the unthinkable, with the implication that everything on which they had relied might need, for its own sake, to be called in question.[18]

FATIMA MERNISSI

A sociologist and university teacher in Morocco, Fatima Mernissi (b. 1940) recently published *Women and Islam: An Historical and Theological Enquiry*, which is as close as one might conceive to being a feminist biography of Muhammad. The root problem of Muslim society today, according to Mernissi, one which the intrusion of the West has forced Muslims to confront, is that women have not been treated as full members of the community.

> Mernissi does not see Islamic gender segregation as an isolated social phenomenon of a religious nature, but as a political expression of a specific distribution of power and authority and an economic reflection of a specific division of labor, both forming a total and coherent social order. When this Islamic segregation is shaken, the coherence of the traditional social order as a whole is put into question, especially if social reform is not able to set up an acceptable new system of values governing male–female relations.[19]

Women may have gained the right to vote in a country such as Morocco, from where Mernissi writes, but they have not gained the right to be elected, she says. Men continue to consider power the privilege of the male and cannot conceive of the need to have women participating in decisions regarding the future. Furthermore, in order to support their position, they appeal to the foundations of the faith of Islam. This accounts for the current surge in Radical Islamist membership, where men find comfort against the inroads of female demands.

To counter these sorts of appeal to religion, Mernissi goes back to the sources to extract a picture of Muhammad as the supporter of women's rights. Mernissi's picture is a mixed one, though. On one level, she seems to say that Islam is inherently male oriented and there is a need to move 'beyond': 'One wonders if a desegregated society, where formerly secluded women have equal rights not only economically but sexually, would be an authentic Muslim society.'[20] But, at the same time, she looks back to Muhammad for inspiration and legitimization. Perhaps this is an attempt to battle Fundamentalist elements (glossed consistently as anti-women) on their own grounds – inter-Muslim apologetics. Muhammad is the champion of women; his opinion is even over-ruled on occasion by God (the implications for the status of the Qur'an in Mernissi's books will be a topic for consideration in the next part of this book), who seems to have been more influenced by the pragmatics of male-oriented power structures than his prophet. The tendency towards reinforcing male power has been further aggravated by male interpreters of the sacred texts, who saw only their own prerogatives at stake and who thought nothing of ignoring Muhammad's intentions of improving the lot of women.

For Mernissi, Muhammad's character reflects precisely what is lacking in contemporary male–female relations:

> Muhammad was a chief of state who publicly acknowledged the importance of affection and sex in life. And, during expeditions, his wives were not just background figures, but shared with him his strategic concerns. He listened to their advice, which was sometimes the deciding factor in thorny negotiations.[21]

The institution of the *hijab*, 'veiling' – here to be taken to mean the entire social system which separates men and women in Muslim countries – became a part of Islam only because of male concerns for their own privileges, and was put in place against the general principles which Muhammad had initiated. Attacks were made on Muhammad because of his private life in which his wives enjoyed a great deal of freedom and authority, contrary to the established practices of society at the time: 'Hurt and weakened, [Muhammad] lost his ability to stand up to 'Umar [pictured here as the spokesman for the male prerogative], and he agreed to the confinement of women. He gave his consent to the *hijab*. He gave his consent to the reestablishment of male supremacy.'[22] Muhammad, for Mernissi, aspired to the ideal society, but the pressures of the situation – a situation into which he had introduced radical change – would not allow his platforms to be maintained. But the equality of men and women and the freedom of women to control their own lives and to be a valuable part of society is what Muhammad stood for, and it is the true core of Islam. The pragmatic value of providing safety for his wives had overcome his principles. Those principles are reflected in the very basis of the religion of Islam, except, it would seem, when it comes to dealing with women. Islam, for Mernissi, stands for the use of the intellect as the means by which good is to be separated from evil. The veiling of women imposed the language of violence and power, whereas individual responsibility was the essence of the society which God wished to be instituted. But the ignorant forces of male power could not accept that responsibility.

> Muhammad put great emphasis on politeness. He himself was very shy. Several verses [of the Qur'an] attest to this aspect of his character, which . . . in the absence of tactfulness on the part of some men of his entourage forced him to adopt the *hijab*. He did not consider that having a house open to the world had to mean that people would invade his privacy. The *hijab* represented the exact opposite of what he had wanted to bring about. It was the incarnation of the absence of internal control; it was the veiling of the sovereign will, which is the source of good judgment and order in a society.[23]

Mernissi's biography is not a traditional one, then. While it covers a great deal of the life of Muhammad, its focus is on the women around him and his attitude towards them. This is no different from, albeit substantially more explicit than, Haykal arguing for the rationality of Muhammad. That is, the point of the biography is made more explicit to the reader; it could well be that, with the rise in general literacy levels, works like that of Mernissi have become more appropriate and more convincing. No longer is it necessary to embed one's ideas so deeply in stories.

'ALI DASHTI

Biographies of Muhammad are, of course, not limited to being written by Arabs. 'Ali Dashti was an Iranian journalist, novelist and politician with a classical religious training; he served in the Senate of Iran from 1954 to 1979. His book, *Twenty-three Years: A Study of the Prophetic Career of Mohammad*, was published anonymously in 1974. He died shortly after the Iranian revolution at the age of about 85; the circumstances are unclear.

Dashti's Muhammad

Dashti's biography presents a full rationalization of prophethood, and is a fairly extreme example at that. Muhammad's experience of prophethood was his own conscience or inner mind speaking to him. Nothing supernatural occurred in Muhammad's life; everything can be accounted for by modern psychology and sociology. Muhammad's infallibility is rejected and thus the 'Satanic verses' are accepted. The Qur'an – Muhammad's book rather than God's – is spoken of as being full of grammatical errors, as should be expected from an illiterate man such as Muhammad, and was taken from a variety of sources. The miracle of the Qur'an lies in its results and its high status cannot be proven by reference to its literary formulation – the poetry of the Persian author Hafez is as untranslatable as the Qur'an but that does not make it miraculous. This comparison is noteworthy because of its Iranian emphasis; Dashti, in fact, accuses the Arabs of being responsible for most of the problems of Islam especially as it is manifested in today's Arab fundamentalism. With the rise of Islam, 'the Arabs did not suddenly lose their materialistic outlook, their inability to think in abstract terms, their unconcern with spiritual matters, and their unruliness and obstinacy'.[24] Only after a few centuries of Islam did the Iranians place 'no value on their nationhood and [imagine] the Hejaz to be the sole source of God's blessings to mankind'.[25]

The lack of rationality in matters of belief has caused the spread of superstition and illusion, according to Dashti. Religion in general is seen to blunt human reason, although there is no reason why this should be so. If people would just accept that Muhammad was fully human then they would understand that everything he did in his life may be seen to fit with general psychological reactions and human emotions. Muhammad's actions must be assessed in the context of the social environment and in terms of their benefit to the community. No standard of firm ethics can be expected from Muhammad. Apparently inhumane principles were used by Muhammad based on expediency and not on consistency with any spiritual or moral principle. Laws from the time of Muhammad are, in today's context, frequently useless and meaningless, as are even some ritual practices, for example the pilgrimage. Concerning Muhammad's wives and various references to them in scripture, Dashti says, 'Every reader of the Qor'an must be amazed to encounter these private matters in a scripture and moral code valid for all mankind and for all time.'[26] In the context of a radical biography such as this, all traditional understandings of both the person of Muhammad and his authority, along with the authority of the Qur'an, are brought into question.

BIOGRAPHY AND REFORM

The examples and the geographical distribution of these biographies of Muhammad from the modern period – both at the beginning and at the end of the twentieth century – could be multiplied substantially. Earlier publications from outside the Arab world – by Ahmad Khan and Ameer Ali in India and Umar Cokroaminoto in Indonesia, for example – indicate that the phenomenon is much larger than that which has been sketched above. In fact, one could also point to a similar use of the biography and ethos of the Shi'ite Imam Husayn ibn 'Ali by Ayatullah Khumayni in the Iranian revolution of 1978–9. Khumayni's appeal to the life story of the leader of the nascent Shi'ite community who was killed by the Umayyad ruler, Yazid, in the year 680 was both vivid and effective. This story is one which speaks to every Shi'ite about the need to rebel against an unjust ruler and to be prepared to sacrifice one's own life for the good of the community. Such actions are seen as redemptive for the individual believer. By alluding to this story and suggesting implicitly that he himself could be viewed as Imam Husayn, Khumayni was able to rally support for political and social reform in Iran despite the overwhelming odds which the clerics faced when confronted by the Shah's power.[27] This paradigmatic use of Husayn achieved literary manifestation, for example, in the book by Shaykh Muhammad Mahdi Shams al-Din called *The Rising of al-Husayn*. Written originally in Arabic by this Lebanese Shi'ite leader, the English translation (published in the wake of the Iranian revolution, in 1985) has a foreword which summarizes well the continuing relevance of religious biography in Islam:

> Imam al-Husayn, peace be with him, created a momentous Islamic revolution, which has continued to live as history has gone by and still provides writers with vitality and inspiring material. Despite the passing of time, it is a revolutionary torch whose light guides revolutionaries and those who struggle to proclaim and support the truth and to resist and oppose the symbols of falsehood. For more than thirteen centuries, writers of different groups, inclinations and ideas have continued to write books and studies about this revolution. Yet neither has its spring been exhausted nor have the streams which flow from it run dry. It is the same as it was at the blessed time it took place in terms of its great significance.[28]

The use of the English word 'revolution' (in Arabic, *thawra*) is significant here and continues throughout the translation. Furthermore, the author alludes to its contemporary relevance:

> From the time of Mu'awiya ibn Abi Sufyan, the Shi'ite Muslim has endured different kinds of persecution, harassment and terrorisation. He has been pursued by the authorities and has seldom felt secure. . . .
> The tragic situation for the Shi'ite has continued for long periods. Out of this situation, under which generations and generations have lived and died, a man has emerged who carries, in the depths of his being, a feeling

of sorrow and a spirit of revolution. This situation has made him keep close to his historical symbols, in the vanguard of which is the revolution of Imam al-Husayn, in particular, and the history of the Imams, in general.[29]

The outpouring of biographical material related to Muhammad and other religious heroes seems endless. There appears to be good reason for this too. The appeal to authority is a necessity, it would seem, and the life of Muhammad is an obvious focal point at which to deal with the issue of reform. The life stories of Muhammad have no authoritative status themselves; they are not the actual source of the *sunna*, although they certainly have relevance in understanding the context of both Muhammad's actions and the Qur'an. Therefore, the subtle rewriting of his biography (as displayed in the examples above) or even the maintenance of the traditional picture (and there are many examples of that in the contemporary world also) does not raise substantial doubts over the basis of Islamic faith, at least on the surface. It is notable, however, that embedded in a number of the biographies, especially the more recent ones, are some far more radical views both of the value of the *sunna* and of the Qur'an as well. And it is to those issues that we will now turn.

4   The authority of the past

Presumed within all biographical treatments of Muhammad as discussed in the previous chapter is the belief that Muhammad has something to say to modern Muslims. Clearly, all Muslims would agree that the story of Muhammad has didactic value; that is, there are lessons and wisdom which can be learned from the actual life story itself. Furthermore, there is fundamental religious inspiration to be gained from reading the story of the founder of the religion, his trials and tribulations, his victories and his defeats. But one question still remains that underlies all of these treatments: to what extent is Muhammad's life, in the sense of all those things which he did in his life, actually binding upon Muslims? Are there simply general principles to be learned from Muhammad's life or are the very details themselves elements which should or must be emulated? One Muslim scholar has expressed his views about this in the following way:

> There is a difference between obedience to the Prophet in his quality of prophet and obedience to him in his quality of *amir* [i.e. leader of the community]. In his quality of prophet he is to be obeyed until the Resurrection, since the Koran is for all times. But in his quality of *amir* he was only obeyed during his life-time. . . . Instructions resulting from his *amir*-ship, will always remain temporary, because circumstances change.[1]

The response to this, representing another point of view, is to say that the two roles cannot be distinguished. Some people appeal to a report in which Muhammad is given to state, 'My community will divide into 73 divisions, all of which will go to hell except one. When asked who these particular people were, he said, "Those who hold the same views as I and my companions have set forth." '[2] The implication clearly is that following the example of Muhammad is the only way by which salvation is assured.

Religion is, as has been mentioned several times before, traditional. It orients itself from the past with a view to the present; it sees authority as vested in and stemming from the past. In the formulations of classical Islam, two things were conceived as fully binding: the Qur'an and the *sunna*, the example of Muhammad. Other sources of authority are in one way or another related to or justified by reference to these two basic sources. Often cited and spoken of in this way are the following legal reference points:

1 *ijma'*, the consensus of the community;
2 *qiyas*, deducing law by analogical reasoning;
3 the *imam*, the divinely guided and appointed living source of authority (appealed to by Shi'ites);
4 the *mujtahid*, one who exercises *ijtihad* or independent reasoning.

Adherence to *hadith* material, the source of the *sunna*, has generally been pictured as maintaining cultural continuity within Islam. But at the same time, it has been argued that the material gathered in the *hadith* reports often hampers attempts to adapt Islam. Thus, questions have arisen: are the *hadith* reports an essential part of Islam? Is it that they are essential but must be subjected to a total reassessment? Are they fully applicable? Or are they totally irrelevant and illegitimate as a source? It is noteworthy that the authority of the Qur'an remains virtually unquestioned, although, as will be seen in Part IV of this book, different ways of interpreting it have been urged and do, to some extent, bring its status into question also.

THE MATERIAL OF TRADITION

In order to clarify the discussions of the status of the *sunna* as they take place in the modern period, it is best to review some basic facts about the formative period of Islam. Information about the life of Muhammad (as found in biographies and in books of *hadith*) is believed by Muslims to have been transmitted from the earliest generations of community members down to the collectors of these books over the following two or three centuries. Such transmissions are documented by what is known as the *isnad*, the 'chain' of transmitters of a report (listed backwards chronologically), while the actual text is known as the *matn*. An example is the following:

> 'Uthman ibn abi Shayba told us that Hushaym told him that 'Ubayd Allah ibn abi Bakr ibn Anas and Humayd informed him that the two of them heard Anas ibn Malik, may God be pleased with him, saying: 'The prophet, may the prayers and peace of God be upon him, said: "Help your brother whether he is an oppressor or an oppressed person".'[3]

Reports such as these comprise the text of a number of books which are devoted to the gathering together of the material. The reports are arranged either according to the transmitter of the report or according to a topic related to the legal framework of Islamic jurisprudence. This latter method of organization proved the most successful, and is the principle employed in the six works which are accepted as being of the greatest significance by the majority of Muslims; these books collected together what were considered genuine *hadith* reports (and, as such, the reports serve as the theoretical basis for Islamic law). The books were compiled by al-Bukhari (d. 870), Muslim ibn al-Hajjaj (d. 875), Ibn Maja (d. 887), Abu Dawud (d. 889), al-Tirmidhi (d. 892) and al-Nasa'i (d. 915).

All the reports in these books deal with what Muhammad said and did, and with what he approved or disapproved implicitly (as indicated by his general behaviour). They are classified into subjects which would appear to follow the legal discussions taking place at the time of their compilation. The chapter headings of a compilation such as that of al-Bukhari reflect the concerns of Muslim life during the formative period of Islam, concerns which go beyond any narrow definition of law and encompass many different aspects. His work starts with what might be considered theological topics: revelation, faith and knowledge. He then deals with various aspects of prayer (Chapters 4–23), followed by charity, pilgrimage and fasting (Chapters 24–32). Thus, the first thirty-two chapters cover what have become the central symbols of Islam, enshrined in the concept of the 'five pillars'. After that, the book covers in Chapters 33–53 general interactions between people (with special emphasis on commerce) and then turns to certain religious concepts such as the merits of the prophets and the Qur'an. Marriage and divorce follow, then a wide variety of topics, ranging from medicine and good manners to apostasy and dreams. The work finishes with 'The Unity of God', thus bringing the sequence to closure. Muhammad, therefore, is conceived to have had some bearing on all aspects of Muslim life, both the personal and the interpersonal, as reflected in this categorization of the *hadith* material.

Historical problems with *hadith* reports

For each individual report, the *isnad*, or chain of transmitters, was considered the guarantor of the genuineness of the text of the report. However, the *isnad* mechanism was, according to Muslims, subject to a great deal of fraud in the early period of its employment. Several methods of evaluating *isnad*s were created, using criteria which dealt in particular with the life and character of the individual transmitters found in the sequence of names. The desire was to document the names in all the *isnad*s which were complete in their testimony to the transmission of the text of the report from generation to generation; the citation of people of high moral integrity who conceivably could have met their cited informants in their lifetimes so that the reports could have been passed on directly was one of the important factors in the assessment of the chains of transmitters.

From a contemporary scholarly point of view, such methods could really only sort out the inept *isnad* fabrications from the less inept. Thus we find, in the collections of *hadith* materials, reports which are clearly concerned with matters of interest to the community in generations after Muhammad but which have been framed as predictions made by him. Theological and legal issues which were discussed in the generations after Muhammad are found to have been resolved during his lifetime; frequently both sides of a given issue will find support in such references to Muhammad. This tendency to fabricate *hadith* reports extended so far as to include reports which could justify the employment of *hadith* reports themselves in trying to settle legal issues, and others which warn against false transmission of reports. The most famous of all such is the following:

> Abu Bakr ibn abi Shayba told us that Ghundar told him on the authority of Shu'ba, and also that Muhammad ibn al-Muthanna and ibn Bashshar both told him that Muhammad ibn Ja'far told him that Shu'ba also told him, on the authority of Mansur on the authority of Rab'i ibn Hirash who heard 'Ali, may God be pleased with him, giving a sermon in which he said that the messenger of God, may the prayers and peace of God be upon him, said, 'Do not spread lies about me! Whoever spreads lies regarding me will enter the fires of hell.'[4]

The forces which attempted to stem the tide of extensive spreading of unreliable *hadith* reports appear to have used the very practice they were trying to condemn in order to stop it.

The authority of Muhammad in classical conception

The fabrication of *hadith* reports arose because of the importance which Muslims attributed to Muhammad in their elaboration of Islam. Muhammad's example became the legal basis for the substantiation of individual items of Muslim behaviour. Historically, Muhammad's practice or *sunna* became a source of law in Islam (second only to the Qur'an) as a result of the desire to introduce both a level of uniformity and a sense of defined authority into the Muslim community. Because of this, the name and, thus, the authority of Muhammad were used to substantiate various legal positions; what a given group of Muslims felt was the correct or appropriate legal practice would at the same time be felt (undoubtedly quite sincerely) to be the practice of Muhammad. Over time, the belief arose that the *sunna* of Muhammad had been revealed by God alongside the Qur'an; the differentiation in terms of revelation was that the *sunna* could not be recited in prayer.

THE *SUNNA* TODAY

The overall question to be raised here, then, is what is the authority of the *sunna* today? Is it felt to give legitimacy to patterns of life, social and ethical codes?[5] Two opposing paths may be used as examples and both will recall the discussion of biographies above. On the one hand, Muhammad is the 'perfect man', a perfect embodiment of the message of the Qur'an. His example therefore must be authoritative, although in modern discussions it is not as common to see this conceived to be the result of actual revelation as it was in classical times. On the other hand, Muhammad is merely human, therefore capable of error and conditioned by his time and circumstances. His example is, as a consequence, not overly relevant or at least not compelling for the modern person. From the Modernist position, this removal of the constraints of Muhammad's example provides an opening for evolution or progress in Islam.

It should be asked, however, why it is that the *sunna* specifically has become the focus of these sorts of discussion, rather than the Qur'an. What is the point of these discussions? For those who enunciate a position which involves extensive questioning of the *sunna*, the aim is to distil Islam down to its essentials and thereby more easily facilitate the incorporation of modern ideals. Those who speak from this position certainly desire the survival of the relevance of Islam; this is true despite the rhetoric of their opponents who picture them as attempting to destroy the religion. Furthermore, one could also say that all parties desire an intensification of Islam. All parties agree with the concept of Islamic law, that is, that religion should say something about legal issues, but they disagree on matters of jurisprudence, that is, the extent to which the decisions of the past are binding on the present. As well, the character of that Islamic law – whose Islam? which Islam? – continues to fragment the various groups.

The Modernist vision is one of an Islam which will more readily incorporate change and, thus, the *sunna* has become the target for criticism and an avenue for aspirations. Part of the reason for targeting the *sunna* is because the custodians of the sacred law were those who were perceived by many reformers as doing the most to prevent the modernization of the Islamic world. Many of the critics came from a lay background; they were not fully trained in the traditional legal sciences of Islam and did not have great admiration for such educational methods. Added to this is the use of Orientalist notions regarding the *hadith* by some reformers. The reports of what Muhammad had done and said during his life were subjected to critical historical analysis by Europeans, especially at the end of the nineteenth century by Ignaz Goldziher, who emphasized the weakness of traditional Muslim evaluations of the material and, even more, the tendentious nature of many of the reports themselves. Some Muslims picked up on this and used these sorts of doubt about the veracity of the material to attack the authority of the *sunna*. This was primarily an Egyptian phenomenon; the criticism of the *sunna* as a whole, however, has much earlier roots, especially in India, where the problem was attacked in more of a theological manner than a historical one.

DISCUSSIONS IN INDIA

The fact that many of the discussions concerning the status of the *sunna* took place in India, and continue to take place in areas distant from the Arab countries, may be significant: the way in which the *sunna* embodies, in a very literal way, Arabian customs may be the jarring point, so that while the Arabs may feel secure in their identity as reflected in the *sunna*, the same may not hold true for those in other parts of the globe. Some have suggested that the more direct contact of Europeans with the Indian population could have been a factor in this movement, at least to the extent that the pressures to adopt European ways were felt more strongly by some people. Also, the Indian heritage of discussions about the *sunna* is long; Shah Wali Allah, an eighteenth-century writer, is famous for his encouragement of a critical attitude towards *hadith*, for example.

Arguments between two contemporary Indo-Pakistani figures display precisely the dimensions of the issues conceived to be at stake in the authority of the past for Muslims. Ghulam Ahmad Parvez represents what is clearly a minority position today in arguing for the illegitimacy of the constraints of the example of Muhammad, the *sunna*. Mawlana Mawdudi is a far more significant figure in terms of Pakistani politics but also of the general Islamic resurgence world-wide. His position, which urges a reassessment of the *hadith* reports which underlie the *sunna* but still acknowledges the authority of the concept itself, is far more widespread than that of Parvez. The discussions between the two indicate the tensions between the different reform positions within modern Islam.

These arguments did not start in India with Parvez and Mawdudi; in fact, the basic issues have been discussed ever since Indian Muslims have tried to grapple with European rule and the relative status of Islam. Sayyid Ahmad Khan represents an example of nineteenth-century Modernist thought, and, on this point, is clearly a precursor to the twentieth-century discussions.

All three of these writers – Ahmad Khan, Parvez and Mawdudi – challenge the traditional religious classes, the *'ulama'*; none of them emerged from the context of the religious scholarly elite. There was, therefore, no way for their views to be declared heretical since the people promulgating the ideas were not subject to expulsion from the religious circles of authority. However, at the same time, 'none of them [is] advocating a situation in which every Muslim can believe as he likes';[6] the communal sense of Islam remains, just as do the limits of the authority of the past.

AHMAD KHAN

Sir Sayyid Ahmad Khan was born in 1817 to a noble family of Delhi. He died in 1898. He joined the East India Company in 1839 and was loyal to the British during the uprising of 1857–8. He urged that all that Muslims needed in India was the freedom to perform public religious rituals; the British should be supported, therefore, as long as they protected the Muslims rather than suppressed them. Ultimately, he saw the need for Muslim separation from the Hindu majority as the only way that an independent India could allow for Muslim survival. Until that end was achieved, rule by benevolent foreigners was a better solution. He was knighted in 1888.

Ahmad Khan may be characterized as a rationalist: he considered the proposition 'religion in conformity with human nature' as absolute. All elements of supernaturalism must be declared false; this would include miracles and the like. Ethics and practices therefore should be based in nature; the law of Islam gives further guidance only. Education about the natural world is essential. His major life involvement was in Muslim education; he devoted his retirement from 1876 on to the establishment and development of the Anglo-Muhammadan Oriental College at Aligarh. Education was the only way in which Muslims were going to be able to recapture their proper status. The school in Aligarh was traditional in the sense that it was a Muslim theological college, but it accepted students from all denominations – Sunni, Shi'i and Hindu – and 'aimed at the liberalization of ideas, broad humanism, a scientific world view, and a pragmatic approach to politics'.[7] Its aim was for its graduates to enter government service and thus eventually pave the way for Muslim separatism within India under this new leadership.

Ahmad Khan and the authority of the past

Deeply influenced by European ideas of history and change, Ahmad Khan embraced the notion that Indian and Islamic history should be studied within the perspective of Western methodologies. He wrote a work on the life of Muhammad (1870), using manuscript sources found in London. This opening of the past to re-examination also led to the possibility of questioning the basis of its authority. This approach was supported by his theological attitude, which saw the need to reopen the discussions concerning very fundamental ideas of Islam; all of this was marked by a severe anti-traditionalism and a strident nineteenth-century modernism. The past interpretations of Islam had become too embroiled in minor details and had lost the essence of the faith. In fact, Muslims had built themselves a structure of law based not upon an infallible source but upon the ideas and attitudes of Muslims from the first centuries of Islam; this was embodied in the *hadith* material.

While the authority of the *hadith* had been established in the past, Ahmad Khan felt that the issue needed to be reopened so as to provide a basis for re-evaluating the *shari'a* as a whole; individual reasoning, *ijtihad*, must be used. This argues, as Sheila McDonough suggests,[8] that nineteenth-century people are as much in touch with determining the norms of Islamic society as was the earlier, ninth-century community which set the standards still followed in Islamic societies. Thus authority itself is not being questioned, only the formulation of it. The only valid *hadith* reports are those which are in agreement with the statements of the Qur'an, those which explain Qur'anic injunctions and those which deal with basic issues not alluded to in scripture.[9]

Ahmad Khan critiques the institution which has maintained the *shari'a* and the idea of that institution itself. Foreign influences are seen as one of the problems in the corruption of the *shari'a*. His aim is the liberalization of Islamic law in the light of modern demands and the rationalization of other elements deemed to be essential.

Underlying Ahmad Khan's ideas is the principle that true religion does not change but worldly affairs do, and the two must be separated. 'In his view,' says McDonough,

> true religion should always be carefully distinguished from worldly affairs. True religion, he said, is unchanging, but worldly affairs are always changing. Originally, the great *ulema* used their personal opinions to give judgments on worldly affairs. This was in itself, he says, a valid thing for them to have done. Later, however, these opinions on temporary issues became identified with unchanging truth. This meant, he says, that the *ulema* were considered law-givers in the same sense as the Qur'an; their human opinions became identified with the will of God.[10]

It is important to notice that in this conception the status of the Qur'an as non-contingent in terms of worldly affairs is not challenged: only the legal structure of Islam needs to contend with change.

PARVEZ

Ghulam Ahmad Parvez was born in 1903 in East Punjab, India. He was raised in a religious home and was deeply influenced, according to his own account of his life story, by Muhammad Iqbal, who pointed out for him the idea of a pure Islam without the centuries of foreign influence. He worked as a civil servant in India, a career seen as developing a concern with definite planning and instruction which he applied to the future of Islam. His first book, a political tract against the Soviet Union, was published in 1926 or 1927, and appeared anonymously because his government job allowed no political involvement. He also wrote articles for Abul A'la Mawdudi's *Tarjuman al-Qur'an* and other magazines. In 1938 he started publishing the magazine *Tulu'-i Islam* ('The Dawn of Islam') which has remained the main vehicle for his ideas since then and is now published in Karachi. He moved to Pakistan in 1948 and worked there as a government official until his retirement. He was a fervent opponent of Pakistan's religious classes, whom he saw as the protectors of elite interests, not of true Islam and true rationality. His audience appears to be mainly well-educated young people, those who have presumably been deeply influenced by the West but are also searching for meaning within their own heritage.[11]

Parvez's basic position

Parvez saw that *hadith* had been treated as a revelatory source by the religious classes of the past. This was not legitimate for him. The *shari'a*, the 'path' of life which Muslims follow, was, as a result of the status given to the *sunna* as a source of revealed knowledge, fundamentally wrong. All of the Muslim past, with the exception of the time of Muhammad and the first four 'righteous caliphs', must be rejected and considered a corruption of true Islam, because foreign influences, especially Byzantine and Persian, had become fully embedded in the *shari'a*. For Parvez, the Qur'an alone can function in taking people from their complacent, destructive ways towards becoming full persons; reason is a base human instinct (but one which demands cultivating certainly) and needs revelation to complete it. At the time of Muhammad, there was the ideal political situation, everything being before God, with absolute authority vested in the leader. To restructure society on its pure Qur'anic foundations was Parvez's goal. In this way, the decline of Muslim civilization – in terms of its power and conditions – would be halted.[12]

Parvez on *hadith*

Parvez's argument has a number of aspects. The Qur'an explains everything that an individual needs and no further source is needed. The Qur'an contains no ruling saying that *hadith* must be followed. Traditionalists claim that the word *hikma* in Qur'an *sura* 2, verse 129, *teach them the book and the 'hikma'*, refers to the *sunna* of Muhammad, but Parvez contends that this word is meant in the general sense of 'wisdom'. Likewise, *sura* 59, verse 7, *Whatever the messenger gives you, take; whatever he forbids you, give over*, relates only to distribution of spoils after battle for Parvez, not to general things which Muhammad proclaimed.[13] Muhammad himself, on the basis of *hadith*, argued against the continuing relevance of his person: 'Do not take anything from me except the Qur'an.'[14] The historical background to this *hadith*, it should be noted, is undoubtedly to be found among those people who in the early centuries of Islam also took Parvez's position on *hadith*, seeing the Qur'an as the only legitimate source;[15] *hadith* and its authority were the result of a compromise, according to Parvez, reached between the rulers and those who wished to uphold the Qur'an alone.

Hadith reports occasionally contradict the Qur'an; for example, the punishment for adultery is 100 lashes in the Qur'an but stoning in the *hadith*. Thus, for Parvez, *hadith* cannot be considered reliable. The unreliability of *hadith* transmission also undermines its validity; any source will be garbled over time (except the Qur'an, which was widely transmitted in uniform style). Subjective judgements were made in the past regarding the transmitters of *hadith*. According to Parvez, even the companions of Muhammad may have erred in their transmissions; this is a position which opposes all traditional theological statements, which hold the companions of Muhammad to have transmitted the material perfectly, limited only by their own perspective on the event being reported.

Furthermore, Muhammad was an ordinary man according to Qur'an *sura* 18, verse 100, and he could have erred. The *hadith* reports frequently include repugnant material, mixing ethical and doctrinal matters. The *hadith* reports have fixed numerous elements of society in a static way in areas not governed by the Qur'an; for example, in the Qur'an it is commanded to give *zakat*, 'charity', which is seen to legislate the principle of 'giving', whereas in *hadith* it is stipulated that such and such an amount should be given. Says Parvez, 'If it had been the will of God that [the rate of *zakat*] had to be $2\frac{1}{2}$ per cent [as the *shari'a* stipulates] until the Day of Resurrection, He would have stated it in the [Qur'an].'[16]

Significance

Parvez's position, like that of other Modernists, tends to separate existence into two. For Parvez, the distinction is between *madhhab*, the ethnic (principally Iranian) elements implemented in revenge for military defeat at the hands of the Arabs (and now to be identified with society), versus *din*, 'religion', which is the Qur'an. His overall platform of urging people to go straight to the Qur'an is one which accommodates the greatest possibilities for change while staying within a traditional understanding of the authority of the scripture; the Qur'an is, after all, far less precise and detailed than the *sunna* as elaborated in medieval Islam, and thus adaptation is far easier to legitimate.

It is interesting to note that much of the emphasis in Parvez's arguments is methodological and theological. Historical questions of whether Muhammad did or did not do such things – questions which have motivated many scholarly studies of *hadith* – seem subsidiary; the concerns are internal Muslim ones, despite the likelihood that Western influence accounts for some of the impetus of the discussions. The overall impact of these arguments, for Parvez, is that the decisions of the past made on the basis of *hadith* are all open to question. Fazlur Rahman points out, however, at least one danger in this position: 'the historical validity of the Koran itself is vouchsafed only by the tradition.'[17] Some may not agree that the Qur'an depends upon tradition to that degree, preferring to see the status of the scripture as vested in the results it has had in society, for example. The point does demonstrate, however, the potential need for those who enunciate such positions to elaborate a full theological vision of Islam.

MAWDUDI

Parvez found his opponent in the figure of Mawlana Abul A'la Mawdudi (1903–79). Mawdudi was raised in a professional and religious family and was educated within a private, family setting in Hyderabad, India. He received no formal religious training but his education was based on traditional Islamic knowledge. He learned Arabic and Persian in addition to his mother tongue, Urdu; later, he taught himself English and read widely in modern thought and science. He became a journalist at an early age and by 1921 was editor of the Delhi newspaper *Muslim*; from 1925 to 1928, he was editor of *al-Jam'iyat*. Both these papers were sponsored by an organization of Muslim scholars known as the Jam'iyat 'Ulama'-i Hind. He started his personal writing, translating and involvement in political activities during this period. In 1933 in Hyderabad, he became editor of *Tarjuman al-Qur'an*, a monthly magazine which became the major vehicle for the enunciation of his views. His early writings of this period concentrated on the conflict between Islam and the Western world view, all being judged on the basis of the Qur'an and the *sunna*.

By the middle of the 1930s, Mawdudi had become more involved in political issues. He argued strenuously against nationalism as being a foreign invention and anti-Islamic, and felt that within India such nationalism would result in the destruction of Muslim identity. In 1941 he founded Jama'at-i Islami, the 'Islamic Society', and remained its head until 1972. The goal of this organization was to effect a change in the life of Indian society, to make it more properly Islamic. However, in 1947, events forced Mawdudi to emigrate to the recently formed Pakistan, and there he vowed to help establish a truly Islamic state; if this state for Muslims was to exist, he argued, it should be an Islamic one. His methods for urging this formation were the involvement of the Jama'at-i Islami in Pakistani politics, constant criticism and inciting to action of the political powers, and a stream of writings all of which aimed to explain the Islamic way of life. This political agitation led to prison terms for Mawdudi, even to the sentence of death for a 'seditious' pamphlet in 1953 (a sentence which was eventually commuted to two years in jail). He remained active in Pakistani politics until the 1970s.[18]

Mawdudi's vision of Islam

Many of Mawdudi's works clearly illustrate his basic view of Islam and portray him as a Radical Islamist. His largest work, *Tafhim al-Qur'an*, is a translation and explanation of the Qur'an in Urdu. Its aim is to present the message of the Qur'an in a clear style for people of today, using the commentary to display how that message is relevant to modern-day concerns.

The fundamental structures of Islam are all based on God, who is in complete command of the universe and to whom all allegiance is owed. The natural order demands that people 'submit', become Muslim; in order to facilitate that, God has sent prophets who bring the guidance which is needed for all humans to govern every aspect of their lives; this guidance is based on the idea of total loyalty to God. Any allegiance to something other than God – nationalism, modernism and the like – is anti-Islamic. Anything other than God which demands allegiance from a person belongs to the *jahiliyya*, the term used in the Qur'an for the non-Islamic (frequently pre-Islamic) ethos.[19] Islamic guidance, the form of divine guidance which is the most complete and totally pure and which directs full allegiance to God, is embodied in the Qur'an and in the *sunna* of Muhammad. The understanding and interpretation of these sources is not vested in the religious learned classes but is available to all by use of personal judgement; those judgements will be made by the yardstick of 'Is it Islamic?' rather than 'Is it rational?', in the manner of many Modernists.

Mawdudi and the authority of the past

Mawdudi argues, on the basis of the Qur'an, that Muhammad is to be taken as a good example for all Muslims at all times. Muhammad as a prophet is inseparable from his being a full example. The very purpose of revelation is to use a person to enact the message; otherwise, God would just send an angel with a book and be done with it. Mawdudi suggests, however, that the idea of Muhammad as an exemplar does not validate slavish adherence to everything Muhammad did. Not everyone should marry an Arab woman, for example![20] It is worth mentioning at this point that, for a Modernist, the issue remains in Mawdudi's position of how to distinguish what should be followed from what should not. Parvez certainly perceived this problem. J.M.S. Baljon notes that Parvez accuses Mawdudi of 'denying tradition' when convenient, as in the length of his beard not necessarily being the same length as that of Muhammad, yet condemning others for doing the very same thing – denying tradition. The accusation is made, in somewhat veiled terms, that those who claim to be able to determine which elements of the *hadith* reports are to be followed and which are to be ignored – as Parvez would suggest Mawdudi is doing – are really claiming for themselves the status of prophethood, in the same manner as Mirza Ghulam Ahmad of the Ahmadiyya.[21] The ultimate answer to this direction of the debate must lie in the concept of *ijma'*, the consensus of the Muslim community, embodied in a more general notion of tradition. The real question, then, is to what extent are twentieth-century Muslims going to maintain those basic elements of the past in their search for modern Muslim identity?

Mawdudi, like Parvez, wants to find an Islamic flexibility which would legitimize change and allow Islam to continue to be relevant to life in the contemporary context. He is concerned, however, that the position which Parvez argued *vis-à-vis* the *hadith* reports, especially where it raises issues concerning their historical value, would eventually be applied to the Qur'an, and Islam would crumble as a result. On the question of whether Muhammad's example should be emulated in all times, he asserts that the Qur'anic evidence argues that it must; the prophetic example is the guarantor of the meaning of revelation and is indispensable to accepting the Qur'an as revelation. The *hadith* reports are reliable as texts because memorization was a highly developed skill among the Arabs and Muhammad was an important person whose words and actions people would have remembered. Certainly, fabrication of *hadith* reports did occur, but this is no reason to dismiss the entire package. The scientific procedures of the past used to assess *hadith* were good but subject to error and were only based upon probability. In an argument typical of Mawdudi's rationalism, the point is made that all of life is based upon probability and we all must use our God-given judgement to decide what to trust. 'Blind imitation', *taqlid*, is no longer sufficient, even though from a traditional standpoint that imitation is the best anyone can attain. To put one's trust in the learned people of the past and follow their interpretations is, from the traditional viewpoint, the appropriate manner of behaviour, rather than to follow one's own insights, which will be sure to be influenced by personal desires and lack of knowledge. This Mawdudi rejects. For him, the learned classes have failed to preserve true Islam and are only acting to preserve their own interests. In Charles Adams' words:

> Mawdudi puts particular emphasis on the argument from probability, saying once more that the fact of a piece of information being only probable does not make it necessarily either wrong or untrustworthy. The proper thing for a serious man is neither to reject all the *zanni hadith* [probable reports] nor to accept them all but to investigate each one individually. The vast majority of *hadith*, because they are *akhbar-i-ahad* [reports transmitted via one *isnad* only] fall into the *zanni* category. One should accept those he is able to prove to be reliable, reject those which he cannot prove, and reserve his judgment about any that fall in the neutral ground between proof and its lack. This he holds to be a reasonable stand and one that is in accord with Islam since Islam is a reasonable religion.[22]

Mawdudi's answer to modernity is rigorous discipline and self-sufficiency along with revolt against inadequately Islamic rulers. His call is to a return to Medina, the perfect political time of Muhammad when true Islam existed and true interpretations were available; the true collectivity of the Muslim community in this period is the final goal of the present time. However, this will only be arrived at by an initial return to the Islamic revolution through quiet conversion as displayed in Mecca. Parvez's call, on the other hand, is to Mecca alone: Islam is internal, and Mecca was the era of pure faith, before time and place constricted Islam in Medina.

DISCUSSIONS IN MALAYSIA

Events in 1986 indicate that the sorts of controversy between Parvez and Mawdudi continue to be vital in other parts of the Muslim world as well. Dr Kassim Ahmad, former chair of the Malaysian People's Socialist Party, wrote a book entitled *Hadith – A Reevaluation*, which was banned by the Malaysian Home Ministry on 8 July 1986, in order to 'safeguard the interests of the people and the country'.[23] Ahmad's position, like that of Parvez, is to reject *hadith* as a basis of Muslim theology and law. He is said to be the first person in Malaysia to put forth such views. The *hadith* are 'sectarian, anti-science, anti-reason and anti-women', Ahmad states. According to available summaries of the book, he poses four main questions:

1 Did Muhammad bring one or two books?
2 Why did the *hadith* take 250–350 years to be compiled and why do Sunnis have different collections from Shi'ites?

3 What factors led to the emergence of the *hadith*?
4 What is the connection between the *hadith* and the decline and backwardness of Islam?

Ahmad's opponents declare that his arguments are the same as those used by other 'enemies of Islam'; the *hadith* are, in fact, essential in order to understand the Qur'an, they say. Ahmad, on the other hand, claims that all the fuss is really a political manoeuvre by his opponents. However, the Malaysian People's Socialist Party has never been a particularly significant force in that country's politics and such reactions are likely to have their motivation elsewhere in this case.[24] That a politician should publish such a book is, of course, significant and indicates that Malaysia, as a nominally (ideologically and sociologically) Muslim country, is going through the process of trying to define itself in terms of a Muslim stance. This may be seen throughout the political structure of the country, one of the legacies of a 1970s' religious resurgence in Malaysia, itself a part of an anti-ethnic-Chinese, pro-Malay-Muslim nationalism. In this country of some 17 million people, 53 per cent of the population are Malay. Most of the Malays are Muslims and they compose the majority of the rural poor. Thirty-four per cent of the population are Chinese; they follow various traditional religious practices and have a high profile in the economy and education. About 10 per cent of the population are South Asians of Indian origin, mostly Hindu. The constitution of Malaysia gives Islam a legally protected status, but the actual implementation of the religion within society varies from state to state. For politicians, then, Islam is a powerful tool in appealing to a large segment of the very mixed population; the problem of a true modernism in keeping with contemporary ideas of socialism is answered, at least in the case of Kassim Ahmad, by questioning the constraints placed on Islam by the *sunna*.[25]

DISCUSSIONS IN EGYPT

The Muslim response to Orientalists, especially the late-nineteenth-century Hungarian scholar Ignaz Goldziher, was more marked in Egypt than in India. Notably, much of the discussion in Egypt centred on certain *hadith* reports which had no role to play in the elaboration of law. Thus the discussion was as much one of principle as anything else. Could the *hadith* reports be trusted? By dealing with a body of material with little impact on the substance of traditional Muslim faith, these Egyptian writers were able to discuss the topic in relative safety.

For the most part, the discussions followed Mawdudi's approach: there was a need to reassess the criteria by which *hadith* reports were accepted, but their value in general could not be doubted. In fact, establishing some traditions as unreliable was an important step along the way towards undermining the legitimacy of *taqlid*, the unthinking acceptance of past authority, which was consistently felt to be the problem.

Rashid Rida (1865–1935) was an associate of the foremost Egyptian Modernist, Muhammad 'Abduh (1850–1905), and was involved in the publication of their Modernist journal *al-Manar*. He argued that following all the traditional *hadith* sciences was simply *taqlid*. The *sunna*, based in *hadith*, is the second root of religion and its foundation therefore needed severe examination. Only the firmest *hadith* reports are to be considered unquestionable, and those were the ones concerned with basic Islamic practices such as the pilgrimage and prayer.[26]

Mahmud Abu Rayya (1889–1970), writing in Cairo in 1958, took the same stance as Rashid Rida. The failure of the religious scholars actually to study the *hadith* reports themselves, rather than their distillations, means they are committing *taqlid*. Only sound *hadith* reports have value and these are very few; all should be judged on the basis of their eloquence (Muhammad's discourse would only be so) and the lack of distortion and alteration. Any false *hadith* reports should not be imposed on society, for they reflect the values of the time and the place of their creation.[27]

Others took the basic arguments further, however. Muhammad Tawfiq Sidqi, writing in the 1890s, for example, argued for the status of the Qur'an alone; God had no need of two books (that is, the Qur'an and the *sunna*), he claimed. The orthodox response to these sorts of claim is to suggest that the *sunna* is a necessity in the roots of law, that as such it is infallible, and that the material upon which it is based – the *hadith* reports – must be considered sound.

AUTHORITY

The controversy over the *sunna* points straight to the heart of views about Islam in the modern period. What is the essential part of Islam that must be maintained and passed on to future generations and what may be discarded as trappings from the past? This is the universal problem for all religions today. All parties in these discussions agree that Islam needs to be revitalized so that its relevance to modern life can be perceived and so that it may be advantageous for individual believers. But what is the proper Islamic way of deciding the basic question of the authority of the past? Does the *sunna* in fact have any authority within an Islamic framework or was this, as Parvez suggests, just a construct created in the past for political expediency? Is the *sunna* a vital part of Islam which has simply become mired in the analyses of the past? These are very fundamental questions about the structural bases of Islam, and the answers to them produce radically different views on what Islam might be in the future. Most answers, when they are in fact produced, seem to urge a gradual reassessment of the past, one which will not produce a severe fracture with practices which are already a part of Muslim society. For some, this is too slow a solution, and for them a more radical approach is needed. Others may try to skirt the issue and instead turn to the Qur'an, the agreed locus of Islamic identity, and attempt a positive formulation of Islam on that basis. The next part of this book will pay attention to the implications of these discussions about the Qur'an.

Part IV

The Qur'an: interpretation and its limits

5   Trends in interpretation

In a manner which would seem to be quite exceptional within the range of contemporary world religions,[1] there is an impressive amount of activity going on in writing works of Qur'an interpretation throughout the Muslim world. The reasons for this must be examined.

Clearly, the search for Islamic identity, for the Islamic answer to the problems of the modern world, has led many Islamic thinkers to make recourse to the original resources of Islam: it has led them back to the Qur'an. This tendency is widespread and not overly surprising; Islam has always been a scripturalist faith and few have wanted to question that basic orientation to the revealed text. Be that as it may, the writing of commentaries on scripture still needs some explanation to account for its prominence and significance.

The field of *tafsir*, the Arabic word for 'commentary', is a traditional one; most of the major Muslim scholars of the past centuries devoted their time and energies to writing such works, generally commenting on each verse or portion of a verse in each *sura* of the Qur'an. The aim for many writers was to explain the text and to explore its ramifications as fully as possible, as well as to make the text understandable. The process was an expression of individual piety on the part of the writer, but it also acted to enunciate each writer's particular view of Islam and its relevance to that age. Therefore, each writer faced a basic difficulty anew (although each worked from the basis of what had been said in previous generations): how to make the text communicate meaningfully within his or her own time and cultural framework. Clearly, explaining the text to Malaysians in the seventeenth century would have required different approaches from those needed in the Arabia of the tenth century.

So, too, is this true in the modern world. The mode of activity of commentary writing has not changed substantially (although the use of certain modern forms – magazines, newspapers – may be noted) and the theoretical demands remain the same: to make the text understandable and relevant.

Modern Qur'anic interpretation is marked, in many of its manifestations, by three inter-related principles:

1 The attempt is made to interpret the Qur'an in the light of scientific reason and methodology. 'To interpret the Qur'an by the Qur'an' is the phrase frequently used to express this, implying the rejection of all the extraneous material provided by tradition in the form of *hadith* reports and earlier commentaries.

2 Following from the previous principle, the attempt is made, through the expediency of interpretation, to divest the Qur'an of all legendary traits, primitive ideas, fantastic stories, magic, fables and superstitions; symbolic interpretation is the primary means for such resolutions.

3 The attempt is made to rationalize doctrine as being found in, or as justified by, reference to the Qur'an.

Overall, it is common to find in modern commentaries an emphasis on the spiritual content of the Qur'an and its guidance. As well, some Modernist approaches are marked by the attitude of viewing the Qur'an as the work of Muhammad's mind, at least to the extent of speaking not of the text descending from heaven in its actual wording (as was classically expressed and is still held in most circles), but of the spirit of revelation being filtered through Muhammad's psyche and thus being expressed within the limits of his intellect and linguistic abilities. As has been remarked by Fazlur Rahman, however, this has not always led to 'historical inquiry into the Koranic revelation on scientific lines, [but] has enhanced the emotional intensity for the Prophet's person'.[2] The ramifications of that have been sketched in the previous part of this volume.

THE BEGINNINGS

The earliest focal point of Modernist *tafsir* activity was in India. Sayyid Ahmad Khan (1817–98) wrote the first major explicitly Modernist commentary, entitled simply *Tafsir al-Qur'an*. His book was directed towards making all Muslims aware of the fact that Western influence in the world required a new vision of Islam, for Islam as it was actually practised and believed in by most of its adherents would be seriously threatened by modern advances in thought and science. Where, therefore, was the true core of Islam to be found? How was its centre to be defined? For Ahmad Khan, these questions were to be answered through reference to the Qur'an, which, if it were properly understood through the use of the powers of reason, would provide the necessary answers. The basis of the required social and educational reforms, for example, were to be found in the Qur'an. By returning to the source of Islam, the religion would be revitalized and the proper future would be secure.

MUHAMMAD 'ABDUH

Generally considered the most significant Modernist figure in the crucial nineteenth-century developments in Egypt, Muhammad 'Abduh lived from 1849 to 1905. He was born in lower Egypt and was educated at the home of Islamic orthodoxy in Cairo, al-Azhar. He studied philosophy with Jamal al-Din al-Afghani and started writing on social and political issues, reflecting many of Afghani's views. In 1877 he started teaching at al-Azhar and shortly after that at Dar al-'Ulum in Cairo. When the British invaded Egypt in 1882 (after the Egyptian army had taken over governing the country from the ruler Isma'il), 'Abduh, who had emerged as a leader of the civilian wing of opposition to Isma'il, was exiled for a time to France along with Afghani. He taught for a period in Beirut, and his lectures there form his book *Risalat al-tawhid*, 'The Theology of Unity', one of the few explicit attempts made to write a Modernist Islamic theology. In 1888 he returned to Egypt and spent the rest of his career as a judge (*mufti*) giving decisions (*fatwa*s) which embodied his Modernist stance. He became the chief *mufti* of Egypt in 1897.

'Abduh's vision of Islam

For 'Abduh, the central problem which had to be faced was the decay of Islamic society.[3] Changing circumstances, unforeseen by Muhammad in forming the Muslim community, had resulted in the status of Islam deteriorating within the community. New codes of law were being imposed, ones which some felt were more compatible with modern economic and social realities. New schools and institutions were emerging throughout society. These changes created a basic issue which had to be confronted: what is it that actually makes Muslim society Muslim?

'Abduh saw change as inevitable and beneficial but also saw the danger of the increasing separation of Islamic spheres of influence and areas controlled by the modern sense of human reason. Bringing these two together became the central platform of his Modernist stance. The simple transplantation of European law, for example, would not provide a viable basis for an Islamic society. Traditional Islamic schools were stagnant and modern schools were devoid of a religious ethos, and this resulted in the further splitting of Egyptian society into traditional and European-influenced sectors.

'Abduh's answer to this dilemma was to link the principles of change to

Islam; Islam would be the controller of change, providing the criteria for selecting what was good and necessary in modern life. His aim was not to convince the traditional learned classes of the need for change, but rather to demonstrate to the more secularly influenced group that it was possible to be devout in the modern age. He hoped thereby that a new learned class would emerge which would be able to articulate the new, revitalized, rational Islam. His book, *The Theology of Unity*, is a good example of the way in which he worked out this position. It is structured in the form of a classical work of theology, starting with epistemology and moving through the topics of God, prophets, revelation and Islam. Throughout the work the emphasis is on logical argumentation, so that the conclusion that Islam is the one true religion must be accepted by all rational people. The logical argumentation, however, avoids the 'excesses' connected to probing into matters declared to be 'unprofitable' for speculation.[4]

Fundamental to this revitalized Islam was the identification of elements in traditional Islam which were consonant with modern thought. Islam was to be seen as a 'civilization' and an activity in life. *Ijma'*, the principle of consensus in law, was to be identified with public opinion. *Shura*, consultation of the elders, was, in this view, parliamentary democracy. *Maslaha*, a legal principle reflecting the ideal of the public interest, could be identified with utilitarianism, in which legal opinion always aims towards the position from which the greatest good will flow.

In order to accomplish his aims, 'Abduh urged a 'return to the sources' in order to reassess them in the light of the modern predicament and with the assistance of human reason. This task is reflected in his Qur'an commentary and has made him the reference point for many Modernist writers, as well as for Fundamentalist groups who highlight his scripturalist emphasis.

'Abduh and the Qur'an

Leading the way for a changed Qur'anic interpretation, 'Abduh struggled against the traditional enterprise of *tafsir*. He argued for the need to make Qur'an commentary available to the people as a whole. The intellectual efforts of the past had made the text 'illegible'; any sense of a distinction between what was important and what was not had been lost. As well, the efforts of the past did not respond to the needs and questions of his day. 'Abduh thus embarked on a commentary that would be minus the theological speculations, the detailed grammatical discussions and the obtuse scholarship which characterized the commentaries of the past. The similarities in impulse and direction to those of the Protestant reformation of Europe may be noted – Luther's Bible translation taking the text out of the hands of the clergy alone and giving it to the common person – along with the impact of the printing press, which became a major factor in the development of Egypt, with the first press established there in the 1820s.

'Abduh's commentary, which was published with the title *Tafsir al-Manar* and was based upon his class lectures and the texts of his legal decisions, is marked by a moderate rationalist spirit coupled with an emphasis on the moral directions for the modern world provided by the spiritual and religious guidance of the Qur'an.[5] The search for knowledge, the use of the intellect, the need for education and the prerequisite of political independence were all to be found in and justified by the Qur'an. What is unknown should be left unknown, rather than embrace the traditional folk tales that attempt to explain it. Any ambiguity which exists in the Qur'an as a result is there for a reason: in order to divert attention away from the material world towards the spiritual. 'If more details were useful, God would have added them.' This, it should be noted, leads to a marked attitude of rejecting interpretations which find modern science in the Qur'an. This tendency is even more pronounced in the work of Rashid Rida, 'Abduh's follower, who completed 'Abduh's *tafsir* after the latter's death. For 'Abduh himself, the Qur'an certainly tolerates (even encourages) scientific investigation, but science is not seen to reveal the true meaning of the Qur'an. References in the text of scripture to telephones and spaceships are functions of the imagination according to 'Abduh and are not based upon sound principles of interpretation, contrary to the opinion of some other prominent writers who will be discussed below.

That the moral point of the Qur'an is the text's highest and ultimate aim in 'Abduh's view may be nicely illustrated by his commentary on the Qur'anic passage dealing with marriage to multiple wives:

> God has made the condition that one keep far from injustice to be the basis for his giving of a law (concerning marriage). This confirms the fact that justice is enjoined as a condition and that duty consists in striving for it.
>
> . . . Polygamy is like one of those necessities which is permitted to the one to whom it is allowed (only) with the stipulation that he act fairly with trustworthiness and that he be immune from injustice. . . . In view of this restriction, when one now considers what corruption results from polygamy in modern times, then one will know for certain that a people . . . cannot be trained so that their remedy lies in polygamy, since, in a family in which a single man has two wives, no beneficial situation and no order prevail.[6]

ABU'L-KALAM AZAD

Azad, who lived from 1888 to 1958, was an Indian politician who was influenced in his modernism by Ahmad Khan and thought highly of his educational ideas. Azad is also said to have been in contact with Muhammad 'Abduh's ideas when he travelled in the Middle East in the early 1900s. He started his career as a journalist and continued to work through journalism for his political causes throughout his life. He was president of the Congress party in India in 1923 and 1940 and was Minister of Education from 1947 to 1958 in independent India. Journalism was his main activity but, in everything he wrote, he manifested his aims concerning the nation of India. He opposed the creation of a separate Muslim state in India and served, from 1937 on, as Gandhi's adviser on Muslim issues. He urged the necessity for Hindu–Muslim cooperation in India in the struggle for independence from the British.

True religion is universal for Azad, echoing a stance of modern Indian pluralism and of opposition to the India/Pakistan split. To recognize this unity is to recognize the unity of humanity. Antagonism between religions has emerged only because people have come to think that they have a monopoly on truth within their own faith; in fact, all religions share in the truth. All religious people should return to the true form of their own religion; this is what the Qur'an instructs. All should submit to God and lead a life of right action according to their own religion. This religious spirit of cooperation reflects his ideals concerning the Indian political situation. All Muslims should return to the Qur'an and the *sunna* and purify their religious tradition from all foreign additions. Care must be taken not to over-emphasize the importance of the ritual and law of any faith, for this is what has produced conflict between religions in the past.

Azad wrote his *Tarjuman al-Qur'an* in the late 1920s as an explanatory translation, but his treatment of *sura* 1 is a full commentary which presents all the basic concepts of Islam. *Din* is what has been given to all prophets everywhere, and this is Islam. *Shari'a* or *minhaj*, used by Azad to refer to the path of Islam, varies with time and conditions, although it is an absolutely necessary and desirable part of all religions.

The Qur'an presents its message as one based in truth, justice and righteousness. Its method of presentation is equally important:

> The primary and the most important feature of the method of presentation followed by the Qur'an is the appeal to reason that it makes. It lays repeated emphasis on the search for truth, on the need of exercising one's reason and insight, of reflecting over the outward experience of life and drawing valid conclusion. In fact, there is no chapter in the Qur'an wherein it has not made an earnest appeal to man to reflect upon everything.[7]

Azad's comments on *sura* 1, verse 4, [*God is*] *the Lord of the Day of Judgement*, illustrates the way he finds the theme permeating the text:

The current religious beliefs had invested God with the characteristics of an absolute and moody monarch who, when he was pleased, showered gifts all around him or, when he was displeased, inflicted dire punishment. Thus arose the custom of offering sacrifices to appease God's wrath and win His favour. The Qur'an's conception of God, however, is not that of an arbitrary ruler who governs according to his moods and whims. On the contrary, the law of divine reward and retribution is a natural law of cause and effect which has universal application. We see its operation in the physical world around us all the time and should therefore have no difficulty in understanding its operation in relation to our spiritual conduct. . . .

So, just as man needs the protection of God the Preserver and the grace and bounty of God the Merciful [as presented in the previous verse of the Qur'an], he cannot do without the divine quality of justice, which makes for organised good life and eliminates, or at least minimises, the elements of harm and mischief.[8]

SAYYID QUTB

Born in 1906 and executed in 1966 for his role in plotting against the rule of Egyptian President Abdul Nasser, Sayyid Qutb was spokesman for the Radical Islamist Egyptian Muslim Brotherhood, al-Ikhwan al-Muslimun, and continues to be a powerful, martyred voice for the movement. He represents, therefore, not the modernism of 'Abduh, but an activist Islamic totalism, one which was initiated by Hasan al-Banna' in 1928 and was a major force in Egypt in the 1940s and 1950s. The thrust behind the Brotherhood was the desire to purify Islam of the corruption of Western morals and influence in general. This was to be done through revolutionary social action, bringing Islamic policies into action in Egypt.[9] Islam was argued to be a comprehensive ideology, one which held the only possible answer to the ills and despair of the day. Islam would and should regulate life totally, and with the full acceptance of the *shari'a* in public life, social justice and political freedom would follow. Reason and public welfare are the operative principles in life, but these must work within the moral principles of Islam alone. Islamic order rests on three basic principles: the justice of the ruler, the obedience of the ruled, and the notion of consultation (*shura*) by which the ruler is elected, controlled and, if need be, deposed. It is thus a political platform, on which all political parties would be outlawed, the law reformed to the *shari'a* and administrative posts given to those with religious education. This type of fundamentalism has proven very popular in many places in the Muslim world, especially among the better-educated young who have rejected both the traditional approach to scripturalism (as manifested in the works of the scholarly elite) and Western modernity. Mawdudi, whose ideas were examined in the previous part of this volume, and Qutb represent the most successful manifestations of the enunciation of this Fundamentalist tendency.

Qutb himself embraced Westernization early in his life but became disenchanted with it, so it is reported, after Israel's formation and after experiencing first-hand what he spoke of as the anti-Arab sentiment in the United States during a stay there in 1949–51. He did not think much of the entire Western way of life:

> I do know how people live in America, the country of the great production, extreme wealth, and indulgent pleasure. . . . I saw them there as nervous tension devoured their lives despite all the evidence of wealth, plenty, and gadgets that they have. Their enjoyment is nervous excitement, animal merriment. One gets the image that they are constantly running from ghosts that are pursuing them. They are as machines that move with madness, speed, and convulsion that does not cease. Many times I thought it was as though the people were in a grinding machine that does not stop day or night, morning or evening. It grinds them and they are devoured without a moment's rest. They have no faith in themselves or in life around them.[10]

These attitudes towards the West and its materialistic trappings are reflected in Qutb's *tafsir* called *Fi zilal al-Qur'an*, 'In the Shade of the Qur'an'. Islam is the 'final, comprehensive, perfect and accomplished message' from God. This Islam is not merely the religious principles of the Modernists, but a full system of life, perfect in its integration of freedom, equality and social justice, one which is in complete accord with the cosmic order.[11] This is expressed in the *tafsir* in the following way:

> *Those who believe and do righteous deeds are the best of all creatures* [Qur'an *sura* 98, verse 7]. This is also an absolute verdict that makes for no dispute or argument. Its condition is also clear, free from any ambiguity or deception. The condition is faith, not merely being born in a land which claims to be Islamic, or in a family which claims to belong to Islam. Neither is it a few words which one repeats again and again. It is the acceptance of faith which establishes its effects on the actual life, *and do righteous deeds*. It is entirely different from the words which go no further than the lips. As for the *righteous deeds*, these are everything which Allah has commanded to be done in matters of worship, behaviour, action and day-to-day dealings. The first and most important of these *'righteous deeds'* is the establishment of Allah's law on this planet, and the government of people according to what Allah has legislated.[12]

Everything outside Islam is, as for Mawdudi, *jahiliyya*, derived from the spirit of barbarism and contrary to everything Islam stands for. Unbridled individualism and depravity are the marks of the modern world and these have culminated in moral and social decline. Islamic society has not simply degenerated; it has, in fact, left Islam and become non-Muslim by negating God's sovereignty and substituting materialism. Modernization and development are plots to colonialize, in material, moral and cultural ways, the entire Muslim world. The reassertion of Islam and the condemnation of *jahiliyya* are the ways to combat this threat. A group such as the Muslim Brotherhood must exist in order to create an alternative counter-society which will produce a model generation of true Muslims.[13]

A study of Qutb's commentary reveals the careful way in which his vision of Islam and society is embedded in the text. A.H. Johns, for example, has looked at the way Qutb treats the story of Moses in the Qur'an.[14] Moses is the 'great figure of moral and social liberation' and provides Qutb with a fitting vehicle for his ideas. Pharaoh is the tyrant ruler of every age who wishes to destroy religion; Moses is the model for all who wish to proclaim the triumph of God's word. Egypt – despite Qutb's emphasis on the whole of the Islamic community, as Johns points out – is the 'cradle' of the world, a green, fertile valley providing all the necessities of life. Threats of jail made by the tyrant to the devotee of God do not cause loss of self-control but only produce demonstrations of the truth of the message, guided by God's power. And this message will resound in the hearts of the people who have lost their faith because of the humiliation they have suffered at the hands of the tyrant. But the remnant of their faith which remains in their hearts will be rebuilt. All of this, of course, while acting to interpret in vivid fashion the story of Moses as told in the Qur'an, is a reflection of Qutb's life itself, of his struggles on behalf of religion against the hypocritical powers of the world – a struggle which Radical Islamists continue today.

Qutb also based his position on an argument about the merits of the Qur'an, and his style of presentation in his commentary reflects this urge. The lack of artistic appreciation of the text on the part of Muslims has meant that the holistic emphasis of the message has been missed; this is especially a fault in traditional commentaries, which took an atomistic approach to the text. The unity of the Qur'an as a book, as reflected in its artistry, is a mirror of divine unity and an image of the cohesive unity of Islam, the religion and social order. The dramatic elements of the Qur'an are a reflection of the drama of human life and the text must therefore be lived for it to be meaningful. Qutb reveals here his own earlier avocation as a belletrist.[15]

'A'ISHA 'ABD AL-RAHMAN (BINT AL-SHATI')

'A'isha 'Abd al-Rahman was born in Egypt in 1913 and was educated in Cairo. She has worked as a professor of Arabic literature in Cairo and as professor of Higher Qur'anic Studies in the Qarawiyyin University of Morocco. She has published over sixty books: novels, short stories, biography, literary criticism and text editions, frequently under the pseudonym Bint al-Shati'.[16]

'Abd al-Rahman's writings always treat the text of the Qur'an on its own terms; she has become a major figure arguing against what is termed 'scientific exegesis' which finds twentieth-century science in the seventh-century text. The aim of scripture, for 'Abd al-Rahman, is spiritual and religious, not historical; the words of the text must always be defined in terms of what they meant to Muhammad and his contemporaries. Further-more, words must be assumed to have been used consistently throughout the text.[17]

'Abd al-Rahman's approach to modern interpretation is not situated as a resurrection of the philological type of commentary associated with classical figures such as al-Zamakhshari (1075–1144), who, although he wrote with great critical acumen with regard to grammar and other technical issues, presents his modern readers with too much unnecessary material which is seen to be a hindrance to understanding; rather, 'Abd al-Rahman pursues a straightforward approach, searching for the original meaning of a given Arabic word or phrase in order to understand the Qur'an in its totality. This process does not involve the use of any material extraneous to the Qur'an itself, except perhaps for a small amount of ancient poetry, but rather it uses the context of a given textual passage to define a word in all its various employments throughout the text. The Qur'an must also be understood in terms of the time and place of its revelation. Neither the history of the Arabs nor that of the Biblical prophets nor scientific topics are to be found in the Qur'an, because providing such material is not seen to be the task of the text. The purpose of the narrative elements of the Qur'an is to give moral and spiritual guidance to the believers, not history or facts. 'Abd al-Rahman's approach is conservative but critical, has often been hailed as a potentially fruitful method for traditionally oriented scholars, and may best be identified as neo-Traditionalist in Shepard's terms. While it has similarities with more-Modernist positions in its emphasis on guidance rather than facts, the absolute emphasis on the text marks it as anti-Modernist. This direction is manifest in 'Abd al-Rahman's other writings, which exhibit quite a conservative view of society[18] and the role of learning; reinterpretation of the Qur'an, for example, should only be done by those who are specialists.

TANTAWI JAWHARI

As has already been mentioned, both Ahmad Khan and Muhammad 'Abduh were intent on encouraging their compatriots to welcome the scientific outlook of the West in order to share in the progress of the modern world. Often this effort involved little more than simply stating that the Qur'an enjoins its readers to seek and use rational knowledge. However, at other times it also involved the historical claim that Islam had developed science in the first place and had then passed it on to Europe, so that in embracing the scientific outlook in the present situation Muslims were only reclaiming what was truly Islamic. A more distinctive trend in *tafsir* emerges also, for example in the writings of Tantawi Jawhari (1862–1940), an Egyptian secondary school teacher who published, among many other educational, religious and spiritualist works, a twenty-six-volume work entitled *Al-jawahir fi tafsir al-Qur'an* ('Jewels in the Interpretation of the Qur'an') between 1923 and 1935.[19]

Jawhari's writings are permeated by two main themes, common to much Modernist writing from the turn of the century: one, Islam is in perfect accord with human nature, and two, Islam, as found in the Qur'an, contains within it an explanation of the scientific workings of the world. God would not have revealed the Qur'an had he not included in it everything that people needed to know; science is obviously necessary in the modern world, so it should not be surprising to find all of science in the Qur'an when that scripture is properly understood. Jawhari also makes reference to the classical notion of the miraculous character or inimitability of the Qur'an (*i'jaz*), which he takes to refer primarily to the content of the text in terms of its knowledge concerning matters which are only now becoming clear to humanity. Since the scientific knowledge contained in the text is proof of its miraculous character, references are found in the Qur'an for numerous modern inventions (electricity, for example) and scientific discoveries (the fact that the earth revolves around the sun).

Jawhari always claimed that his exegesis was no more far-fetched than the traditional legal approach to the text. Scientific exegesis stems from a view of the Qur'an and the *sunna* as providing all the knowledge that people would need. The Qur'an therefore anticipates modern science. What is more, as a tendency in interpretation, this exegetical approach has an honourable pedigree with classical precedents, for example in al-Mursi (d. 1257), who found astronomy, medicine, weaving, spinning, agriculture and pearl-diving mentioned in the Qur'an.

The tendency to scientific interpretation (although now markedly out of date in the actual scientific information provided in the instance of Jawhari himself) has become widespread and is often used as a popular means of trying to convince non-Muslims of the divine nature of the Qur'an and Islam. A startling example which was recently in circulation in Turkey in an English-language publication (and thus presumably designed for tourist/ non-Muslim consumption) comments in the following manner on Qur'an *sura* 66, verse 6, 'The fire whose fuel is men and stones':

> A vast amount of energy lies locked in the nuclei of matter. In accordance with Einstein's equation, $E = mc^2$, it is known that a single gram of matter, if converted into energy, would yield energy equivalent to that contained in 2500 tons of coal. If the atoms of men and stones could be converted directly to energy, we would be faced with inexhaustible amounts of fuel.
>
> The real aim of the sacred verse, then, is to direct our attention to this fact. In other words, it intends to teach us the truth hidden in the essence of matter.[20]

Apologetics is not the only accomplishment of scientific exegesis, however. Muslims have found their faith enhanced and renewed through exposure to these sorts of claim. Typical is the following testimony from an Egyptian doctor of pharmacy, published in a 1991 textbook of world religions:

> Some of the statements in the Qur'an had no meaning at that time, 1400 years ago, but they have meaning now. For example, 'We have created this universe and we have made it expanding.' 'We have made the earth look like an egg.' Such statements cannot come from just an average person living 1400 years ago. Among ancient Egyptians, ancient Syrians we cannot find this information. I started to believe that someone was giving the knowledge to Muhammad. I'm not a very good believer – don't ask me to believe just because there is a book. But this information cannot come from any source except One Source.[21]

The argument against this type of approach, as enunciated by some Muslims, is that it suggests that the language of the text was not that of Muhammad and his times; that is a lexically unsound approach, according to these critics. The word *samawat* (literally 'heavens') translated as 'universe' in the previous quotation, for example, would have conveyed a certain meaning to Muhammad and his followers which would have been quite different from what is conveyed by the word 'universe' today. As well, of course, such interpretations are opposed to the common Modernist idea that the Qur'an's value is in its spirit and general guidance and that it is not a source-book of facts.[22] The ever-changing scientific ideas of the nineteenth and twentieth centuries should not be identified with the unchanging value of the Qur'an, say many opponents. Shabbir Akhtar points out that these 'arguments, if indeed that is the appropriate term for them, carry conviction only with devotees'. Rarely, Akhtar notes, is the criterion of scientific consistency applied throughout the text:

> If the koranic claims tally with scientific views, it is cause for celebration in the religious camp; if not, it is declared either that the beliefs currently prevalent in the scientific community are, conveniently enough for Muslims, erroneous or else that secular scientific truths are irrelevant to judgements about the truth of revealed claims. ... For to accept a consistent application of the criterion is, as the religionists themselves vaguely sense in some moods, in effect to impose a very exacting demand upon revelation. Is the Koran's authority, then, dependent upon its being able to achieve conformity with current scientific scholarship?[23]

TAFSIR IN OTHER PARTS OF THE ISLAMIC WORLD

The writing of commentaries goes on throughout the Muslim world, not just in India and Egypt. Ibn Badis (1889–1940) was a famous Algerian Modernist reformer who turned to *tafsir* to provide a vehicle for his ideas about contemporary political questions.[24] In Iran, Sayyid Muhammad Husayn al-Tabataba'i (1903–82) published an Arabic work entitled *al-Mizan* ('The Balance'), some of which is available in English translation, which presents a totalist vision of Islam with a neo-Traditionalist flavour.[25] In Indonesia, people such as Ahmad Soorkatie presented the Modernist ideas of Muhammad 'Abduh in the form of Qur'anic commentary embedded in lectures given in the Malay language.[26]

TRENDS IN INTERPRETATION

As should be apparent from the above discussions, books of Qur'anic interpretation have become a vehicle for the spread of diverse ideas in the Islamic world. Support for various conceptions of Islam is found in the scriptural text along with many passages which are deemed to have the answer to the dilemma faced by Muslims and their faith in the modern world. All such works urge the relevance of Islam to the modern day, but it must be an Islam properly understood; and that is where the differences between the approaches begin to appear. We have seen Modernist, Modernist with a universalist emphasis, Radical Islamist with literary and scientific emphases, as well as neo-Traditionalist with a philological bent, all of which compete with their own definitions of what is essential in Islam.

It is notable that the discussions and presentations thus far illustrated have not raised fundamental questions about the nature of the Qur'an and how that is to be understood in the modern world. We turn to this in the next chapter.

6   Types of critical approaches

DIFFERING INTERPRETATIONS

Practical examples of looking at texts from the Qur'an provide the best illustration of the issues which are at stake in talking about types of Muslim critical approach to the Qur'an, the problems which they raise and the limits to which they will go. Here is a good exercise for the reader: read the following three sections of the Qur'an[1] and consider their problematic aspects within the modern context. Assume the stance of a Modernist Muslim: what do you perceive as problematic? Assume the stance of a Radical Islamist: what is your response to a Western perception of difficulties with these texts?

The first example

Sura 56, verses 11–24:

These will be
Those Nearest to God:
In Gardens of Bliss:
A number of people
From those of old,
And a few from those
Of later times.
(They will be) on Thrones
Encrusted (with gold
And precious stones),
Reclining on them,
Facing each other.
Round about them will (serve)
Youths of perpetual (freshness),
With goblets, (shining) beakers,

And cups (filled) out of
Clear-flowing fountains:
No after-ache will they
Receive therefrom, nor will they
Suffer intoxication:
And with fruits,
Any that they may select;
And the flesh of fowls,
Any that they may desire.
And (there will be) Companions
With beautiful, big,
And lustrous eyes, –
Like unto Pearls
Well-guarded.
A Reward for the Deeds
Of their past (Life).

This sensual picture of the rewards of heaven can evoke a variety of responses. For the Modernist, such portraits are potentially objectionable for what they imply about the relations between the sexes and for their material imagery in dealing with the rewards in the hereafter. Furthermore, Modernists will react to the Orientalist–missionary suggestion that this afterlife picture is somehow unspiritual (with the insinuation that Christianity has a more elevated view). Such a position may want to propose that the picture is to be taken as mythic, that it is expressed in a language which would appeal to those at the time of Muhammad and urge them to convert and 'submit' to the will of God. Such a resolution of the perceived problem suggests a certain relativization of the Qur'anic message in history: that parts of it may only be directly relevant to a certain age.

Others, of the Radical Islamist persuasion perhaps, will insist that the passage reflects a reality, but that the reality is spoken of in metaphors and similar figures of speech. The 'Companions', often translated less euphemistically as 'fair maidens' (in Arabic: *hur*), are not maidens at all, but priests who will minister to all, for example. The accuracy of the text, therefore, is not to be relativized but is to be reinterpreted in a fashion amenable to the modern spirit – but the reality is still there in the text.

Traditionalists have no difficulty with such a passage: there is no reason to suggest that the hereafter will be the least bit different from its literal description as provided by God in the Qur'an: the only evidence which we have for the nature of the afterlife is provided in scripture, and God will have described it accurately and will have designed it in a manner pleasing to him and to humanity.

The second example

Sura 23, verses 12–18:

Man We did create
From a quintessence (of clay);
Then We placed him
As (a drop of) sperm
In a place of rest,
Firmly fixed;
Then We made the sperm
Into a clot of congealed blood;
Then of that clot We made
A (foetus) lump; then We
Made out of that lump
Bones and clothed the bones
With flesh; then We developed
Out of it another creature.
So blessed be God,
The Best to create!
After that, at length
Ye will die.
Again, on the Day
Of Judgment, will ye be
Raised up.
And We have made, above you,
Seven tracts; and We
Are never unmindful
Of (Our) Creation.
And We send down water
From the sky according to
(Due) measure, and We cause it
To soak in the soil;
And We certainly are able
To drain it off (with ease).

The previous passage suggested a situation about which humans have no evidence other than scripture. Here we deal with issues which relate to our knowledge of the natural world: birth, the notion of heavens ('tracts') and rain. From some perspectives this information must be either right or wrong. For the Radical Islamist all this information must correspond to scientific knowledge, when both are properly understood. The very translation of the words relating to birth, for example, already reflects the assumption that the words were understood at the time of revelation in a semi-scientific fashion which agrees with current investigations into the stages of development of a foetus. More problematic, perhaps, is 'seven tracts' or 'heavens', but even there, various layers in the earth's atmosphere can be identified with these seven. It is significant to note the extent to which the proper interpretation of these passages – according to this view – would only have become clear to Muslims in the latter part of the twentieth century.

Scripture, for the Radical Islamist, cannot be relativized to the point of saying that the text reflects the state of knowledge of the world at the time of Muhammad, as would be the position of some (more radical) Modernists. These passages, Modernists might suggest, do not attempt to tell us of the facts of the world. Rather they reflect basic ideas that all suggest the glory and power of God; the importance of the text lies not directly in what it says but in what it points to.

For more traditional thinkers, any apparent conflict between such passages and modern science only illustrates the changing nature of scientific knowledge. The reality of the world is in the accurate description given by God. When observation of the world is done properly (and investigation is generally to be encouraged), the truth of the Qur'an will be borne out.

The third example

Sura 4, verse 34:

Men are the protectors
And maintainers of women
Because God has given
The one more (strength)
Than the other, and because
They support them
From their means.
Therefore the righteous women
Are devoutly obedient, and guard
In (the husband's) absence
What God would have them guard.
As to those women
On whose part ye fear
Disloyalty and ill-conduct,
Admonish them (first),
(Next), refuse to share their beds,
(And last) beat them (lightly);

But if they return to obedience,
Seek not against them
Means (of annoyance):
For God is Most High,
Great (above you all).

It is unlikely that any other passage in the Qur'an has created more furore in the contemporary period than this. Pivotal is the word *adribuhunna*, here translated as 'beat them (lightly)'; other translators soften the tone further with 'chastise them'[2] or other similar sentiments. The Arabic word is used commonly to mean 'beat' and there is no doubt that traditional Islam has taken the word in that physical sense. For the Radical Islamist, there are two options, depending on the view of society and family values. First, the passage could be taken literally but with emphasis placed on the legal requirements which are associated with the passage: for example, the necessity to 'fear' disobedience would be taken very seriously. The strict application of the passage could then be argued to be 'for the woman's own good', to protect her from herself. Implicit here (and, in fact, frequently made explicit) is the rejection of what is considered to be a Western norm of family and male–female relations that would suggest that using physical force to ensure obedience is necessarily wrong. Some would claim that the ethical code promulgated by this passage under this interpretation is in fact the way things should be; the failure to embrace a proper (that is, Islamic) family structure is what has led to the degeneracy of the West – the 'spare the rod, spoil the child/woman' syndrome.

However, another Radical Islamist position on this passage would be to reinterpret the word 'beat them'. Phrases such as 'chastise them' leave the text of scripture intact, and suggest that Islam has its own standards which are, in fact, better than those encouraged in the West but are fully respectful of the responsibilities of both men and women.

It is Modernists who encounter the greatest problem in dealing with this passage. To declare the law appropriate for an earlier time, appropriate for a stage when people were still evolving morally, is to suggest that even the legal contents of the Qur'an are contingent upon history; only the basic religious impulse of the Qur'an – the existence of God, his omnipotence and majesty – remains as the everlasting message of scripture.

This position of the contingency of the law is not accepted by many among the vocal promulgators of Islam in the contemporary period, for the absolute nature of the law of the Qur'an is generally considered one of the central tags for the identification of Islam. Consider the following recent news item, entitled 'The "Four-Man" Woman':

She is one of Pakistan's most sought-after models, an aspiring actress and a national beauty queen. Anita Ayub was in the Philippines last year [1989] competing in the preliminary round of the Miss Asia–Pacific pageant when she reportedly made some fateful remarks. She was quoted as saying that Muslim women should be allowed to have four spouses, just as Muslim men can take four wives at any one time. The statement horrified the Pakistani mission in Manila. A tearful Ayub was forced to withdraw from the beauty contest.

There was more trouble back home. Outraged Pakistanis accused her of preaching immorality. Under Islamic law, it is a crime for a woman to have intimate relations with a man other than the one husband she is allowed to have at one time. The penalty: death by stoning.

In January, 22 high-powered Islamabad lawyers demanded that the beauty queen clarify her statement. But Ayub was not forthcoming. Terming her alleged Manila statements 'illegal, immoral and highly irresponsible', the advocates then lodged a complaint with the local city magistrate. The case is still [April 1990] being heard.

Ayub is up against no less than holy writ. The Koran sanctions polygamy but limits it to men. It stipulates that all four co-wives be treated equally. . . .

As for Ayub, the beauty queen is keeping an uncharacteristically low profile these days. She herself is unmarried and, perhaps not surprisingly, there is little talk of any marriage in the air.[3]

If one overlooks the gratuitous and sexist remark at the end, this report points out what many Muslims fear, especially those of the Radical Islamist persuasion, though the feeling is more widespread than that: relativizing the Qur'an to the standards of today – in this case conceptualized as equality between men and women – will lead to immorality.

THE ISSUES AT STAKE

There are two main questions which arise in modern discussions of the Qur'an that illustrate, in a more abstract fashion, the limits to which these critical approaches may go in dealing with the contingency of the text. The first begins from the question of the miraculousness of the Qur'an and moves into the general question of its rationality, and the second raises the question of the difference between legal and moral regulations. Both of these are interconnected, one leading to the next, at least in the thought of some people.

The miraculousness of the Qur'an

Classically, the doctrine of the *i'jaz* ('miraculousness', 'inimitability') of the Qur'an has been seen to assert the totally non-contingent nature of the text: it is fully divine and the language is that of God. The Qur'an is the word of God *per se*. It has no relationship in its form to the passage of historical time. It literally descended from heaven, having been written on the pre-existent divine tablet. Any conflicts created by this attitude to the ultimate authority of the Qur'an have always been solved by pointing to the limits of human knowledge – we simply do not fully understand.

Some Muslims have urged a somewhat modified understanding of the miraculousness of the Qur'an. In general, this conviction may be viewed as an aspect of the anti-supernaturalism and the support of rationalism which has already been noted, especially in discussions of Muhammad's biography. But the question remains: to what extent can anti-supernaturalism be taken regarding the Qur'an without destroying Islam? And underlying that question is always a second one: what is Islam?

A frequent response, as in the case of 'Ali Dashti, is that the miracle of the Qur'an lies not in its form, which is the most important aspect of the classical statements on the matter, but in the divine guidance which the book provides and the success which it has had. Thus the elevated, divine status of the Qur'an (and therefore in one sense its miraculousness) is maintained but the traditional interpretation of each doctrine is done away with. This then allows two further thoughts for some people: a removal of all other supernatural elements *within* the Qur'an and a questioning of the precise understanding of the non-contingency of the text.[4]

Another common tendency is to conceive the Qur'an not as revealed literally but as installed in Muhammad's heart and then spoken through the human faculties of the prophet. The language, therefore, is Muhammad's, although it is still possible to hold that this is ultimately God's word also.[5]

The impetus behind these discussions rests with the basic drive of the Modernist movements: the need to modernize, reform and rejuvenate Islam. The means to do this is found in removing what is envisioned to be the stumbling block: anti-rationalistic ideas along with norms which are perceived as not being in keeping with modern society.

In addition, there has been the methodological influence of the historical-critical method as developed in Europe. Basic to this method are a number of assumptions, all revolving around the scientific rational impulse – that history moves by causality and that those causes may be determined and studied. History must be studied according to the laws of reason, for that is the way the world works. Religion is nothing special in this regard: it is like any philosophy or literature and like nature itself. It must be coherent, logical, and capable of being incorporated into an understanding of human history. Biblical scholarship of the eighteenth century enunciated this stance quite plainly, for example in the case of Johann Salamo Semler who published a study of the Bible between 1771 and 1775 which 'called for a purely historical-philological interpretation of the Bible, in the light of the circumstances surrounding the origin of the various books, without any concern for edification'.[6] Detached from theological and philosophical restraints in the nineteenth century under the impact of Schleiermacher, Biblical studies 'made impartial and objective research the ideal'.[7] The end result of this for many twentieth-century scholars is summarized in the following:

> The only scientifically responsible interpretation of the Bible is that investigation of the biblical texts that, with a methodologically consistent use of historical understanding in the present state of its art, seeks via reconstruction to recognize and describe the meaning these texts have had in the context of the tradition history of early Christianity.[8]

For the most part, the impact of the historical-critical method has been slow to be felt in the Muslim world, at least within the study of the Qur'an. The reasons for this lie within the traditional discussions concerning the nature of the Qur'an which have just been mentioned. It must be remembered how much Muslims perceive to be at stake here: the existence of Islam classically depends upon the miracle of the Qur'an. Thus, for those who have determined that this is the route to go, caution is a continuous feature. Assessing the basic character and nature of the Qur'an must be accomplished first, and that means raising questions of the rationality of the text and of its relationship to historical fact. The issue still lingers, as the following examples will show, of just how far Muslims can go in pursuing these questions while still remaining Islamic.

Rationalism and the Qur'an

Establishing the rationality and the anti-supernaturalism of the Qur'an has been a frequent aspect of discussions concerning the scripture and it goes hand-in-hand with a Modernist perspective on the nature of the text. But how far can this be pushed? An interesting example of the Modernist argument is found in the work of Muhammad Abu Zayd of Egypt who wrote, in 1932, a book called *Guidance and Instruction in Interpreting the Qur'an by the Qur'an*. The book caused such an uproar when it was published that it was seized by the police. The commotion continued to such a degree that some conservative religious scholars attempted to declare Abu Zayd a non-Muslim and to have him separated from his wife; this is an interesting example, by the way, of the method of 'excommunication' within Islam, since there is no clergy and no communion from which someone may be excluded. The centrality of legal matters to the definition of the status of being a Muslim is well illustrated in such a case. A Muslim woman may only be married to a Muslim man, so if Abu Zayd has, by virtue of his writings, declared himself to be a non-Muslim, then he is no longer legally entitled to be married to his wife. He was able to fight against this charge successfully in the courts. He was then accused of corrupting the young.

Abu Zayd starts with the observation that Muslims have strayed far from the Qur'an and no longer follow its dictates. This is the cause of the present condition of Muslims, and it has been provoked by the classical commentators who have layered law and theology on top of the text, so as to obscure its true message. The whole role of traditional knowledge in interpreting the Qur'an is rejected, for it is full of mistakes and people's prejudices.

A new interpretation is called for, one that will follow the principle of the Qur'an interpreted by the Qur'an (a common Modernist expression, as already noted) so that nothing will distract one from the text itself. All that is needed in approaching the Qur'an is 'our general understanding of the way in which God works in the world around us and in human society'.[9]

As a result, all supernatural elements in the Qur'an are to be eliminated through the processes of interpretation. Satan ('anyone who magnifies himself above his right') and the angels ('the principle of orderliness and customary habit in the world') are spiritualized; the heavenly journey of Muhammad is rejected, with the Qur'anic reference taken as referring to the *hijra*, Muhammad's emigration from Mecca to Medina.

A similar approach is taken with certain legal passages. The text as it stands is by no means rejected; it means precisely what it says when it is 'properly interpreted': cutting off hands as a punishment for theft does not apply to a single theft but to hardened criminals whose instrument of thievery, their hand, should be removed. This is not an attempt to say that the law does not apply, but is similar to a commonly heard idea regarding polygamy, for example, which asserts that when all the texts on the subject are taken together, they add up to a prohibition of the practice – all wives must be treated equally and that is beyond the capabilities of any man.

What marks this type of commentary, therefore, is the extent of its anti-traditionalism and full rationality; in no way, however, does it actually challenge the authority of the Qur'an itself. No passage of the scripture may be neglected; everything has some relevance.

MUHAMMAD AHMAD KHALAF ALLAH AND HISTORICAL SPECIFICITY

Rationality or anti-supernaturalism, then, is one area where the limits of interpretation are confronted; the desire to see scripture as fully in keeping with reason can only be taken so far before those who maintain a more traditional view of Islam raise their objections. Another area where these limits are confronted is seen in the relationship between the text and historical reality, often spoken of in terms of the conflict between 'truth' and 'reality'. Muhammad Ahmad Khalaf Allah (b. 1916), in a thesis submitted to Cairo University in 1947, brought this issue to prominence in the Islamic world. While the issue had been broached by others before him, especially his teacher Amin al-Khawli (1895–1966),10 in Khalaf Allah's instance, public reaction was fairly rapid. He wrote that the prophetic stories in the Qur'an were not historical as such but kerygmatic: that they were being repeated for their moral/religious aims, and were repeated in different forms according to Muhammad's needs in a given situation. They were therefore contingent upon history even in their aims. This is the distinction between what may be termed 'truth' (in a spiritual sense) and 'reality' (as reflected in historical fact).

Khalaf Allah was accused of 'atheism and gross ignorance' and had to rewrite his thesis several times before it was accepted; it was published in 1950–1 but he was subsequently forced out of his university teaching post. Traditionally, all the stories of the Qur'an have been seen to be of equal value and to be of a historical nature. This position raised a number of questions in the modern world, however. What of stories which did not seem to be in agreement with other, earlier sources? For example, in the Qur'an Haman is presented as Pharaoh's minister while in the Bible he is a minister to the Persian king of a much later period. What is a modern Muslim to believe? Are the facts of the Qur'an all necessarily true historically and all other sources false? How will this attitude work in conjunction with the historical-critical method which clearly values older sources over newer ones? One of Khalaf Allah's concerns was apologetic: how to save the Qur'an from the attacks of the Orientalists who continued to cite all these problems within the text.

Khalaf Allah's resolution of the problem was to say that the concern of the Qur'an is to employ striking literary expressions through which psychological and religious truths are expressed. Its concern is not necessarily with historical or material truth (that is, 'reality'). Literary genres, specifically the historical-literary, parable and allegory, have been employed within the Qur'an to embody these spiritual truths. The aim of the Qur'an was to 'admonish and exhort', not to instruct in history. Hence, information about time and place are generally missing in the Qur'anic narratives.[11]

The examples of Abu Zayd and Khalaf Allah raise issues about the limits to which Muslims are prepared to take reinterpretation of the Qur'an. Rationalism, the underlying principle of the historical-critical method, is fully applied in these cases in order to resolve the problems perceived within a general Modernist tendency. Neither writer actually doubts the authenticity of the text of scripture, only whether the words themselves are to be taken as intending to convey precisely what it has been traditonally thought that they say.

A CONTEMPORARY RESPONSE

At the time of publication, much of the response to Khalaf Allah's work dealt with it by saying that the author was using history as a criterion of truth higher than the Qur'an, something which no Muslim could accept. The ultimate truth of the text of scripture exists, in these responses, *a priori*. A more subtle argument is made by Shabbir Akhtar, who does not raise the example of Khalaf Allah specifically but certainly deals with the principle in his book, *A Faith for All Seasons*. He approaches the problem as though it had only affected Christian study of their scripture; he may well not be aware of the extent to which Muslims have already broached these questions. Regardless, the case of the 'sophisticated Christians' (as an example he cites Richard Swinburne) provides a cautionary tale for Muslims, according to Akhtar, who wish to maintain their faith in the light of philosophical approaches to scripture. Akhtar points out that it was Darwin who made it so necessary for Christians to distinguish between 'the false non-religious husk and the concomitant true religious kernel'.[12] This has gone to the extent now that Christians are willing to talk about false cultural trappings in which scripture has expressed truths for ignorant people of the past. Some statements of the Bible, or the Qur'an, in this view, may be taken as 'unempirical or false'. For Akhtar, the problem with this is: how can one be sure that the underlying religious claims, which have been embodied in these false statements, are necessarily true? There is no way, he contends, to 'distinguish in any unquestion-begging way . . ., between the religious message presumed to be true and the culturally specific incarnation presumed to be false'.[13] After entertaining several possible ways around this problem – that God incorporated errors in scripture to keep us on our toes, or that apparent errors are matters which are simply beyond human reason – he concludes by saying that any concession to the idea of false claims in scripture must be resisted. If this is not so, then while

today we disown what we take to be factually erroneous, perhaps tomorrow we will reject apparent moral anachronisms – such as scriptural claims about the relatively low status of women or the impropriety of deviant sexual behaviour, not to speak of the occasional questionable doctrine about the nature or activity of the Deity.[14]

Revelation, for Akhtar, is an all-or-nothing affair; that is the only way to construct a philosophically defensible Islam. Watering down the doctrine of the non-contingent nature of the text too far will lead to there being no defence against claims that the entire basis of the religion may be false.

THE CONTINGENT NATURE OF QUR'ANIC LAW

Khalaf Allah did not confront the question of the nature of the law; in fact, he studiously avoided raising the issue. Neither did he question the divine nature of the Qur'an. It should be noticed that, from his perspective, it is not necessary to question the Qur'an's status as the actual word of God; God may reveal speech which does not have the intent of providing historical facts, but it may still be conceived of as God's word.

But when this kind of approach confronts the legal parts of the Qur'an, further issues arise. Are the laws contingent, that is, applicable only to the time of Muhammad? Are they embedded in the history of the early Muslim community or are they expressions of the eternal will of God?

FAZLUR RAHMAN

Fazlur Rahman (1919–88) was Director of the Islamic Research Institute in Pakistan from 1962 to 1968 but, after pressure from conservative elements in that country, was forced to leave; he became professor of Islamic Thought at the University of Chicago in the United States and achieved a reputation of being one of the great scholars in the field.[15]

Rahman was a fervent Modernist. In approaching the text of the Qur'an, he wished to differentiate legal regulations from moral regulations, the former being contingent, the latter non-contingent. Legal rulings must be considered binding in a moral sense even if not in their literal wording.[16] Much of the law of classical Islam has been wrongly formulated because the jurists ignored the moral ideal behind the text and the words were read as literal legal enactments, according to this view. The Qur'anic acceptance of slavery, a form of ownership of people which has fallen into disrepute under the impact of modernity, is treated in the following way by Rahman:

> As an immediate solution, the Qur'an accepts the institution of slavery on the legal plane. No alternative was possible since slavery was ingrained in the structure of society, and its overnight wholesale liquidation would have created problems which it would have been absolutely impossible

to solve, and only a dreamer could have issued such a visionary statement. But at the same time every legal and moral effort was made to free the slaves and to create a *milieu* where slavery ought to disappear. . . . Here again we are confronted by a situation where the clear logic of the Qur'anic attitude was not worked out in actual history by Muslims. . . . These examples [also including women and wine], therefore, make it abundantly clear that whereas the spirit of the Qur'anic legislation exhibits an obvious direction towards the progressive embodiment of the fundamental human values of freedom and responsibility in fresh legislation, nevertheless the actual legislation of the Qur'an had partly to accept the then existing society as a term of reference. This clearly means that the actual legislation of the Qur'an cannot have been meant to be literally eternal by the Qur'an itself.[17]

It is not only on legal topics that Rahman has approached the Qur'an in this manner, although it is in that area where the extent of his demythologization becomes most clear. The psychological intention of the text as opposed to the descriptive meaning is frequently employed as a principle in his work, *Major Themes of the Qur'an*. God's power, humans being predestined, intercession in the afterlife, divine punishment of humans, and the existence of genies are all interpreted not for their literal sense but for what they were driving at in terms of motivating humans towards the proper attitude regarding God, life and creation.

This position fits into an overall neo-Modernist stance, according to Rahman himself, one which recognizes the complexities of life as opposed to the fundamentalist idea of everything (especially Islam) being 'simple'. Once again, it is the history of Islam which has taken Muslims away from the proper understanding of the Qur'an; the text of scripture itself is still a perfect reflection of standards as they should be, as long as it is properly understood. Rahman blames the educational institutions developed in the early Muslim centuries for the failure to appreciate the true import of the Qur'an. The educational system created what it called the Qur'anic sciences along with the legal structures of society. It separated these religious sciences from the rational or secular sciences (Rahman traces this division back to al-Ghazzali, d. 1111) and, with the growing disrepute of the latter studies, Islamic civilization fell into stagnation. The worst consequence of this was the rejection of Islamic philosophy, which could have kept open ways of inquiring into the foundations of Islam, but was unable to. No longer was the Qur'an treated as a 'vibrant and revolutionary document'; rather, it became 'buried under the debris of grammar and rhetoric', a trend reaching its apex with the notion that only super-commentaries – that is, commentaries on commentaries on the Qur'an and *hadith* written by the scholars of the past – could and should be written.[18] The way Islam can free itself from this burden of the past is by studying history critically, in order to comprehend how the impetus of the Qur'an has been understood in the past and how Muslims have interacted with it. Thereby, the essentials of the faith may be differentiated from that which has simply attached itself unnecessarily.

PUSHING THE 'LIMITS'

Some Muslims would take this further or perhaps even question the very presuppositions of the historical-critical method and approach the issue in a totally different way. We have seen in the previous part of this volume, for example, how Fatima Mernissi perceives the Qur'anic attitudes towards women: that they reflect male ideas put in the mouth of a male God. The law of the Qur'an – through language – is culturally conditioned from beginning to end.

The same sense emerges from the writings of Mohammed Arkoun.[19] In dealing with the Qur'an specifically, Arkoun pays attention to the historical development of interpretation of the scripture, a process which serves to establish *how* the Qur'an takes on meaning in the Islamic context. This then leads to the observation that, from within the modern context, Muslims are attempting to read the Qur'an as if modern reason was in all ways identical to the linguistic shape of the Qur'an and Muhammad's epistemological environment. The logic of the Qur'an, from Arkoun's perspective however, is a poetic logic rather than a rational logic. Ironically perhaps, it is precisely because the Qur'an is written with this poetic logic that it can be read by those who wish to do so as if modern rationality were reflected in it. For Arkoun, of course, the Qur'an conveys a mythical discourse rather than a historical one, but by that very fact it allows a historical interpretation.

The necessity today is, for Arkoun, to approach the Qur'an with today's categories which are composed of the totality of the human sciences. The selection of these forms a refrain – even a litany according to one of his reviewers: ethnology, anthropology, history of religions, psychoanalysis, semiotics, and with human consciousness to be viewed mythically, historically, socially, economically, politically, philosophically, morally, aesthetically, religiously and so forth. The aim of this is to discover the way in which all elements of culture are bound ideologically with history. All of human existence is founded upon and created by history and only through the realization of this can the past, present and future become clear. This is demythologization at its extreme.

As an example of what this might mean in a practical sense, an issue of law is useful. For Arkoun,

The basic difference between the Qur'an and the *Shari'a* is that the first makes use of contingent data in order to emphasize the relationship between God and man and to fill men's minds with a consciousness that there is a world beyond this world of events, values, norms and possessions. All this is clothed in mythical language and structure which opens the way to problems rather than excluding them. The second, on the other hand, systematizes, within the framework of a code of law, the pragmatic solutions that were adopted at an early period. It is understandable, then, why it is wrong to call norms that have been included in this code and perpetuated by an inflexible teaching Islamic.[20]

The Qur'an then does not provide answers but problems, ones which must be struggled with in human life.

It is the aim of Arkoun's method to get 'outside' the dualities of contemporary discussions which still deal with the understanding of the world in historicist terms. The historical-critical method is not the answer for the needs of the Muslim consciousness in the latter part of the twentieth century.[21]

This approach does not even seem to entertain the idea of Rahman's moral ideals within the Qur'an. Could it be said that Mernissi and Arkoun get to the point of challenging the authority of the Qur'an text itself? In traditional understandings of 'text' and 'authority' they clearly do. Their understandings seem to call for a re-expression of the Qur'an – one that stands, however, completely within the *Muslim* ethos. Mernissi wonders, for example, if an Islam which gave women freedom could really be called Islam at all:[22] it might be termed post-Islamic, I would suggest. One of the reasons for the radicalness of these positions is that neither writer stands within the now-traditional historical-critical method, although the reasons for this may well be different in the two cases. Mernissi's use of the feminist interpretative framework brings her face to face with the historical issues, but there is a tendency in her writing to step back from what might seem to be the inevitable conclusion. Arkoun, on the other hand, wishes to change the very terms of the discussion and eliminate the duality of the discussion between contingent and non-contingent, for example, for those terms imply that there can be human knowledge which is outside the framework of historicity and language. From this perspective, 'limits' to critical approaches make little sense, for the limits are those imposed by linguistic structures; the deconstruction of those limitations is the entire purpose of the exercise.

Part V

Ramifications of modernity in Muslim daily life

7   Feminism's 'new Islam'

The subject of the examination thus far in this volume has been the intellectual discussions conducted in Muslim circles over the past two centuries which have attempted to enunciate an understanding of the basis of Islam in its contemporary context. Certainly not all Muslims have taken part in the actual discussion of these issues sketched earlier, but they all do, in fact, have a position on them, whether they enunciate it or not. How the Qur'an is to be understood and how Muhammad is to be conceived are the hermeneutical fundamentals upon which Islam is based, and even those who simply follow what has 'always' been thought on these topics are taking a position within the debate. Furthermore, it is clear that some of the discussions taking place today have had a profound impact upon the face of Islam as a whole, not only in its intellectual and ideological formulations but also in its practical ramifications.

Muslims as individuals are far more concerned with the implementation of their religion as a vital part of their lives than they are with the theoretical understanding of the underpinnings of their faith. Islam is a 'simple' religion, says a popular phrase in Radical Islamist circles, and it is not in need of these intellectual discussions. And yet the point remains that the basic principles which surround the intellectual conceptualization of the fundamental elements of Islam – the Qur'an and Muhammad – make their mark even in the basic aspects of modern Muslim daily life, despite these claims. One area in which this may be demonstrated revolves around the discussions dealing with women's place in modern Islam, especially as this reflects further issues concerning the entire structure of Muslim society.

Obviously enough, women comprise about 50 per cent of all Muslims. While all Muslims, male and female, would agree that Islam stands for and aspires to a single religion regardless of the sex of the adherent, the sociological facts speak otherwise. Islamic society has both encouraged and allowed specifically female modes of religiosity within the overall framework of the religion. This is the result of a number of factors which could be termed both negative and positive. The exclusion of women from the power structures of institutionalized Islam, along with the specific religious requirements for women, have jointly brought about specific female-oriented ramifications. Islamic law, with its enunciated roots firmly in the Qur'an, has instituted a social system based upon the presumption of an extended family grouping within a patriarchal system. This has existed, quite successfully, in creative tension with the notion of the Muslim *umma*, the community within which all are one under their relationship to God. Within that overall social system with its assigned roles for women, certain women-focused religious activities have emerged. Feminists would say that women have sought to build a world to replace the one from which they have been excluded.[1]

The modern age has had a severe impact upon the social system of Islam, as has already been noted several times in this volume. At the same time, the place of the family within that social system remains central to much of the sense of Muslim identity.[2] Not surprisingly, therefore, issues of women in the context of the family receive what might be considered a disproportionate amount of attention in the discussions of Islam in the modern context. This focus on women is not necessarily an apologetic response to the pressures of the day, for, as was just suggested, family roles have always been fundamental elements of Islamic identity. Furthermore, the question of women's roles in society is an enormous problem at the present time for a number of reasons. The traditional assumptions about the way in which family life is structured are being questioned daily, not simply by intellectuals and Western-educated individuals but by the urban masses as well. The transition from rural to urban society, resulting in overcrowded cities, mass transit, poverty, unemployment and all the other characteristics of modern life, has meant a severe disruption in the roles played within the family. Education has also exaggerated the problem, not just by creating a reflective group of people who recognize that knowledge is power (only to have that insight rendered meaningless frequently by their failure to achieve any significant social power despite their education), but by radically changing the social structure. Both men and women have tended in recent times to delay marriage while education was being undertaken. This has resulted in the emergence of a group of people not even contemplated in the traditional Islamic social system: unmarried adolescents. The jurist's social system can only conceive of the female child and the married woman.[3]

Therefore, the question emerges: what is to be done to make Islam relevant and even helpful in this new situation? It is the discord felt between modernity and the traditional religious forms that is stimulating the need for change. It is not that accusations are necessarily being made that Islam is somehow 'at fault', but rather that attempts are being made to draw on traditional religious resources to find the answers for today. Islam has functioned, through its divinely authorized social system, to provide identity for its members by drawing the social boundaries of individual existence in relationship to other members. Under the pressures of today, the identity provided is no longer coordinate with the aspirations of some people, many of whom are women, or at least the straightforward answers of the past no longer prove sufficient in responding to modern questioning. The issue of women, then, is one which displays, in very vital form, the implications of the intellectual debates which have been discussed earlier in this volume.

TRADITIONAL PATTERNS OF WOMEN'S RELIGION

In practice, women have been excluded from substantial areas of Islamic ritual. Menstruation, while not implying a ritual contagion in Islam, serves as a barrier to ritual performance for the woman concerned. Thus, while men have nothing to fear from women being present at prayer, for example, the ritual status of a woman would be on public view if her attendance at public worship were to be required whenever she was able to attain a ritually pure state. Islam, therefore, instituted what might be termed a paternalism, generally excluding women from public performance of the daily prayer for the benefit of their privacy. Other reasons for this exclusion are frequently proffered, especially within apologetic presentations of Islam. Women prove a distraction to men at prayer, some claim, not allowing the believers to concentrate fully upon the divine; praying separately, then, is advantageous for both sexes. In addition, women have other responsibilities within the family structure which preclude their participation in regularly scheduled events; this explanation for different ritual requirements according to the sex of the believer is also common in Jewish apologetics.

The result of this separation has not been the establishment of rival female institutions in which women may perform their rituals separately. Rather, in many places in the Muslim world, specific popular religious practices often associated with mysticism and saint worship (something which many Muslim reformers have targeted as 'non-Islamic') have emerged, activities which exist outside the male-dominated institutionalized forms of Islam. Such cults are seen to have provided women with a sense of solidarity and independence from men. The magical aspects of this worship, manifested in trances, vows and oaths, are viewed as powerful tools in the relationship between men and women. Fear is often seen to be instilled in men because, through their wives' activities in these saint cults, power is believed to be held over a man's virility and fertility.[4]

Another popular Islamic institution, resulting from the legal institution of ritual cleansing and from the practicalities of society, is the public bath.

Here, women gather within the intimacy of their own sex and participate in social circles beyond their own kin grouping. Observers have noted that women emerge with a significant form of power from this structure because they are able to move between family groupings in these contexts to a far greater extent than men are able in male-oriented situations. The 'inside track' on social, political and economic movement is available to women, frequently then to be shared with their husbands within the confines of their own homes, a factor of some value in domestic power arrangements.

SECLUSION

Seclusion of women has become the most firmly lodged image of Islamic society in the Western popular imagination. That is an image which reflects a reality and a basic principle of the Islamic social system, although the precise form which it takes varies with geographical location (and implied cultural differences), social status and a variety of other factors. The honour of the family is what is traditionally seen to be at stake, although this is critiqued frequently by pointing out that it is the male sense of honour which is being protected on the assumption of a female tendency towards independence and uncontrolled sexuality which must be restrained. The behaviour of the female is therefore to be controlled to preserve male honour.

The word used to refer to this seclusion varies: *hijab* and *purdah* both refer to a principle which frequently becomes manifest in the clothing of women and which is expressed more accurately in contemporary terms as *al-ziyy al-Islami*, Islamic modest dress, denoting a covering of the hair and an obscuring of the shape of the body. Seclusion as a whole is an ideal which is aspired to but cannot always be afforded. For women in total seclusion, servants are required in order to run errands; this was and is beyond the means of many families. As well, in the modern world, it is often easier for a woman to find a job to provide a source of income for her family than it is for an uneducated man to do so; this means that a woman will, of necessity, be thrust into society outside the home. In rural societies, the restrictions on the movement of women were always of little consequence: the family, within which a woman has no restrictions, was seen to extend throughout the village and thus freedom of movement (required for women to participate in agricultural tasks and so forth) created no difficulty.

The concept of seclusion has produced a great deal of debate in Islam, with some people stating that seclusion is not a part of the religion, and others saying that it is. As is frequently the case, this is as much a matter of definition of words as anything else. The total veiling of women – taken as a way of implementing a 'movable seclusion' – is not stated as a requirement in the Qur'an and, on that basis, is often suggested to be simply a cultural trait and not a part of Islam. This is true only, however, if attention is paid to the outer form of clothing alone. Veiling is, in fact, the logical (although, strictly speaking, perhaps not necessary) outgrowth of various Qur'anic statements taken to their limits. Full veiling institutes the Islamic attitude towards social interactions between men and women in its fullest degree, in a manner that ensures that violations are extremely difficult. Of course, why this specific issue – the seclusion of women – should be the one that Islamic jurists took to such an extreme formulation as compared to other aspects of Islamic law may well be questioned. Overall, however, one of the implications of the symbolism this seclusion suggests is that women are conceived to have power while being (out of necessity in the male view, it would seem) restrained at the same time.

In terms of legal standing in the Islamic system, women's rank, logically enough, reflects the assumptions of the social structure. This is how it should be, after all; a social system is unlikely to function well if the confines of that system do not allow a group of people to assert the status which the system grants. Thus the Qur'an establishes that the testimony of two women is required to equal that of one man (Qur'an *sura* 2, verse 282). The portion of a woman's inheritance is less than that of a man (*sura* 4, verse 11). Divorce is allowable upon the woman's instigation only for a set number of reasons, whereas a man needs no specific pretext at all. A great deal of concern is displayed over establishing the lineage of children; while men are free to remarry after divorce, women must wait (while being supported by their ex-spouse) to see whether they are pregnant. The male rules the house in all matters: the religion of the male is presumed to be the religion of the entire household; thus a Muslim male may marry a Jewish or Christian woman, but a Muslim female may marry only another Muslim (*sura* 5, verse 6). A man may marry up to four wives at a time, but a woman may marry only one husband. Discipline (*sura* 4, verse 34) and sex (*sura* 2, verse 223) are the prerogatives of the male to which the female is subject.

There is a sense conveyed in the Qur'anic statements which suggests that women will not wish to cooperate in society and will need to be coerced. For example, that a woman must wait a certain period after divorce or after becoming a widow in case she should be pregnant so that paternity may be firmly established would seem necessary only on the assumption that a woman would wish to hide relevant information about her sexual liaisons. Additionally, Fatima Mernissi has argued that Islam is based not on the misogyny which characterizes Western society, but on the fear of heterosexuality.[5] Mernissi's view is echoed by other writers, for example in the fiction of Alifa Rifaat.[6] The women of these short stories, poignantly illustrated by the unnamed woman of the title story 'Distant View of a Minaret', at first seem to crave for more love and life and yet they are constantly disappointed by their male companions. As a result they find their only solace in performing the worship of God within the context of female religious practices.

It might be possible to invert Mernissi's argument and say that this guarded attitude towards sex is precisely what is appropriate. The Islamic social system is set so that women will not distract men from worship and are themselves then forced to worship for their own comfort. But the objection would remain that this had been accomplished at the price of the full human-ness of both sexes.

MODERN DEMANDS

'Equality' has become a catchword world-wide when speaking of women's issues. The concept is slippery, however, and needs a clear definition in order to be able to anchor an analysis. In most cautious feminist discussions, equality does not mean 'sameness', as some opponents might try to suggest in their attempts to trivialize the issues. Equality refers to potentiality of human-ness, a self-determination for 'life options'. These are issues of opportunities, not roles. The experience of gender is the most prominent aspect in the discussions of the issue. The social process of the internalization of gender is seen to determine the limits in achievement of human-ness which, it is suggested, we are all entitled to. There is, in Judaeo-Christian-Muslim society in general, a relationship between power and gender, and gender internalization is a means of control to the advantage of patriarchy; gender roles and the control involved thereby serve to the advantage of the already established prerogatives of the male in society. Mernissi summarizes this aspect of the problem of being a woman: 'Why can't I stroll peacefully in the alleys of the Medina?'[7] That is, the very fact of being a woman in society limits the activities which she might wish to undertake, and these activities are ones which men take for granted in their lives.

Another term frequently used in discussions about women is 'status', but that too is rather evasive conceptually. 'Status' frequently seems to imply that there are some given categories into which social roles may be categorized and that these may be used to compare social functions. This, however, ignores the fact that different social systems reflect different assumptions; looking only at something called 'status' therefore views only the superficial manifestations of a social system and not its underlying structure, which would seem to be far more of a key to understanding.

Notably, a great deal of the analysis of gender structure is specific not to Islam itself, but to patriarchy in general as a world-wide phenomenon. And Islam's assumptions certainly reflect a patriarchy within its society. Thus, from some points of view, Islam has not allowed the possibilities for women which it has for men; if the social system of Islam reflects the best possible solution for all, then why is it that a woman cannot stroll around the Medina, to repeat Mernissi's phrase? 'Inferiority', a popular idea of what the complaint of women is all about when it comes to discussion of their status, misses the point: Mernissi argues that the issue is really one of subjugation. That is, society does not reflect ideological positions regarding women which are necessary to its functioning as such, but rather reflects assumptions about power structures.

The idea of the complementarity of the sexes is often used in talking about the Islamic understanding of the roles of men and women in society; the concept is especially popular in Radical Islamist circles whose approach to the Qur'an necessitates the continuation of legal differentiation between men and women. Women have their role to play in society as mothers and home-makers while men shoulder the responsibilities for maintenance of the family in financial ways. The question from this position is not one of 'subjugation' or 'inferiority', but rather 'natural order' reflected in the concept 'equal though different'.

The complementarity notion suggests that women want and need to be isolated in society and do not wish to play a more active role in the world at large; this, the theory suggests, is 'natural'.

> The functions of the husband and wife are quite distinct, and each is entrusted with the functions which are best suited for his or her nature. The Qur'an says that God has made man and woman to excel each other in certain respects. The man excels the woman in constitution and physique, which is capable of bearing greater hardships and facing greater dangers than the physique of woman. On the other hand, the woman excels the man in the qualities of love and affection. Nature, for her own purpose of helping in the growth of creation, has endowed the female among men, as well as the lower animals, with the quality of love to a much higher degree than the male. Hence there is a natural division as between man and woman of the main work which is to be carried on for the progress of humanity. Man is suited to face the hard struggles of life on account of his stronger physique; woman is suited to bring up the children because of the preponderance of the quality of love in her. The duty of the maintenance of the family has therefore been entrusted to the man, and the duty of bringing up the children to the woman. And each is vested with authority suited to the function with which he or she is entrusted. Hence it is that men are spoken of as being the maintainers of women and women as 'rulers over the household and the children'.[8]

Furthermore, any of the so-called restrictions on women resulting from this assessment of the situation are argued to be for the benefit of women themselves, and are seen to be based upon the differences in nature between men and women, differences which are, after all, at the bottom of any assertion about complementary roles.

> Possessors of beauty are comparatively few in number, and the natural course of life changes the appearance of those and renders them homely. When women without the veil mingle with men, the favorable attention of the latter will be drawn only to beautiful women and charming young girls. Naturally unattractive women would be considered undesirable, and this would result in their being cut off from society and companionship. This would mean, on the one hand, a decrease in the population and, on the other hand, since men are not always able to procure beautiful wives, that their attention would be drawn to handsome children. Therefore if one looks at this question from the standpoint of reason and justice, he will see that the veil prevents corruption.[9]

Objectors to the theory of complementarity note that it is based upon an idea of men and women having such antagonistic wills that the two sexes need to be separated into different spheres of competence, since, it would appear to be fundamentally assumed, they could never cooperate. These assumptions, however, are cultural constructs according to feminist critiques; they are ideas which are designed to preserve male power and to control female power, and, implicitly at least, have become embedded in the Qur'an and the *sunna*. Interestingly, the Islamic view of society according to this vision of complementarity is based upon a strong notion of women's power as something which must be restrained.[10] It is, therefore, a part of the double notion that pervades gender construction in Islamic society (and perhaps generally): woman as powerful along with woman as needing to be dominated. There is a further irony and a contradiction involved in this. Women achieve a secure sense of gender identity through restrictive and oppressive controls over their being (and especially their sexuality); the very controls which are imposed have the result of identifying women strongly *as women*.[11]

ISLAMIC ANSWERS

Most writings by Muslim women on Islam and the 'problem' of women emphasize that the problem is, in fact, not a religious one; religion is the answer, not the problem or the source, according to these authors.[12] Religion, as found in the Qur'an and the *sunna*, provides a definition of the 'natural order' of things and the proper implementation of this will lead to the satisfaction of all people – men and women – in society.

One very popular expression of this, a traditional one in Christianity also, is to see the husband's relationship to his family as a mirror of the relationship between God and humanity.[13] This is a cosmic reflection, then, of the natural order of things, which is also echoed in the biological differences between men and women: woman as nurturer, man as aggressor. The basis for this is, of course, to be found in the divine affirmation that two sexes have been created – not one, but two. If God had intended each human being to have been capable of all dimensions of life, he would have created only one sex. Furthermore, Muslim apologists point out, women are not burdened by the Biblical image of being the source of evil because, in the Qur'an, the story of Adam and Eve does not reflect those ideas in its retelling. Likewise, the 'gender' of God is not an issue. Arabic only has two grammatical genders and their separation is, to a large extent, arbitrary. The fact that the noun for God is grammatically masculine does not reflect, according to this view, any pre-eminence of the male. This kind of apologetic trend dominates the discussions and there seems to be little evidence of any attempt at a feminist theological vision of Islam. The questions may well be broached at some point in the future: what would it mean, for example, for all people, male and female, to be members of a community of *Muslimat* (that is, the feminine plural of *Muslim*, itself the singular masculine form) rather than the *Muslimun*, as it is now expressed in the masculine plural form? Writers such as Riffat Hassan[14] come the closest to raising such issues, but this is generally done in academic circles and even then does not lack an apologetic tendency. It may well be, however, that women writers will emerge, writing in Arabic, Persian or Urdu, who do not feel the same needs to challenge 'Western misunderstanding' about Islam, and who will start to define a female theological vision.

THE USE OF THE PAST

The most frequent observation made, rarely without patronizing overtones, is that the 'status of women' given in the Qur'an is a vast improvement over that of the pre-Islamic period. Before Muhammad, female children were subject to infanticide, women were the possessions of men without any rights, and so forth. 'In the days of Ignorance, it was common among women to freely mix [in] public. They exposed any part whatsoever of their [bodies] to the public gaze. It was not considered indecent or immoral.'[15] The coming of Islam empowered women, to the point that their legal rights exceeded those of European women until very recently. This view, however, is opposed by other writings which speak of the power and prestige that women had in the pre-Islamic period, which men, under the guise of a (mis-) interpreted Qur'an, have gradually removed.[16] 'A'isha, the wife of Muhammad who is a frequent source of authority in *hadith* and famous as a leader of a revolt in early Islamic times, is the central role model of such perspectives. Even more radical approaches to the material suggest that Islam itself was responsible for the movement away from women's power (a power sometimes even linked to a matriarchal system) and towards the present position of subjugation.[17]

From the perspective of a historian, it may be pointed out that all these views are based upon selective citation of evidence. Women in pre-Islamic Arabia may be portrayed as powerful and active, or as tyrannized with no power, according to which facts are presented. What must be remarked, therefore, is that all of these approaches are attempts to remythologize society with a more productive vision. That vision will be one which embraces the ideals of the group concerned: for the Radical Islamist, the 'myth' of empowerment via Islam; for the feminist, the 'myth' of women's potential gradually removed by men (either as embodied in Islam or as 'misinterpretation' of Islam). The problem remains that these are myths which are easy to deconstruct.

Classical Islam itself provides a mythological picture of pre-Islamic society, as was pointed out in Volume 1 of this book. By Islamic definition, *jahiliyya*, the age of ignorance, is everything that Islam has come to remove. The picture found in classical texts, therefore, of a matriarchal society in which women played an active role is a part of the Islamic myth itself. That is how Muslim males of the ninth and tenth centuries pictured a society which was at its lowest point morally and socially: women in control! This myth stands in tension with the other aspect of the pre-Islamic mythic picture, which sees Islam as providing moral growth from the pre-Islamic period – thus the picture of the improvement in women's rights – but the aspect of women in this mythic story provides only part of the story. Rather, this myth provides a general evaluation of the overall legal accomplishment of Islam. Each element of Qur'an law has become embedded in narrative detail as evidence of this transformation accomplished by Islam. In a typical development of structural myths, both aspects exist side by side, acting to control society and justify present practice; each probably has its origin in a specific historical situation and reflects the aspirations or frustrations of a certain period. Their continued existence together poses a problem only for modern historians who tend to isolate one element from the narrative structure in the desire to create coherence out of the historical records, and for those who wish to remythologize.

HIJAB IN THE MODERN CONTEXT

The preservation of the home as an Islamic focal point of life becomes a central defence of much of Muslim life in the modern world, especially in geographical areas which are not predominantly Islamic. With secular society encroaching from all sides, the home becomes the representation of an Islamic paradise, an oasis of divinely structured society located in a context fully awash with everything Islam rejects. *Hijab*, in this mode of behaviour, becomes a home-oriented activity. Once again, this person-alization of religion may be suggested to be both the result and the cause of this particular interpretation and way of being Muslim. One's own religious behaviour becomes the most important aspect of the exercise of Islam, rather than its communal manifestation, and seeing its implementation as limited to one's own home (at least in the religion's social implications) seems to act as a line of defence. The possibility exists of taking the personalization of Islam to its fullest extent and, in the specific case of the Islamic notion of the seclusion of women, speaking of the necessity of the *hijab* of the heart as the only requirement. While such interpretations certainly have a heritage in Islamic mysticism, their role in legitimating personal behaviour in secular-ized society should not be underestimated.

WOMEN IN THE MUSLIM *UMMA*

An oft-quoted statement of Egyptian feminist Nawal al-Sa'dawi is worth repeating; she is arguing against Radical Islamist suggestions that the natural place for women is in the home and that corruption will occur if women are encouraged to seek employment outside the home:

> These men [who make this argument] ignore the fact that the majority of women in Egypt (80 per cent or more) are peasants and have never worn the veil. They leave their houses every morning to work with a hoe in the fields or to carry loads of dung or pails of water on their heads. Does this mean that these men think these millions of Egyptian women have abandoned their femininity which nature has given them, and are exposed to moral corruption or lack of protection for their religion and honor? If so, why have these men kept quiet? . . . Why have they not demanded that the peasant women be protected inside the homes and not be made to go to work in the fields?
>
> Since we have not heard of any of them making such a demand, does that mean that they consider these millions of Egyptian women corrupt in their morals or lacking in femininity or having little honor and religion? Or do they believe that femininity and honor are qualities enjoyed only by a small minority of Egyptian women?[18]

Sa'dawi's argument brings two points to the fore. One, powerful feminist voices do have a presence in the Islamic world, despite the media presentations. Two, and more salutary, Sa'dawi reminds us that, in fact, for the vast proportion of Muslim women, the 'crisis' of modernity has brought a negligible effect. Radical Islamist arguments are, to a large extent, phenomena of the urban centres, where social and economic factors loom as the stimulus behind the rejection of feminist argumentation regarding the place of women in society. For women in rural areas, the Islamic social system remains intact and coherent, rendering men and women significant social actors within their own particular fields of control. Those fields of control, it is to be remembered, regulate relations not only within each sex but also between them: men and women establish power structures both over each other and among their own same-sex groupings.

The reality of the situation in the urban context cannot be denied, however. The (re-)assertion of male authority over women, characteristic of Radical Islamism, and in many cases the assertion of the state's power to control women's activities are symptoms of economic and social pressures resulting from the radical restructuring of society taking place in many areas of the Muslim world.[19] The economic roles of women in society have changed substantially and the declaration of Radical Islamists that women belong in the home is a cry of sorrow to return to the safe values of the past as elaborated in the Qur'an and the *sunna*, where men's economic and social roles were firmly established. That is a phenomenon not unique to the Muslim world, of course. Neither is it only a matter of male concern. When there are few, if any, roles for women to play in society outside the (traditionally) prescribed ones, the (re-)adoption of things such as Islamic dress or the rejection of feminist ideology may be taken as an expression of women's own frustration at social and economic conditions.

8 The practice of Islam

In the previous chapter, we examined some of the ramifications of the modern period as they have been felt within the structures of Muslim family life and as specifically related to women. In this chapter, subtly altered understandings of the basic ritual activities of Islam will be discussed as illustrating some aspects of the transformations which are taking place in modern Muslim faith. Once again, these changed understandings and interpretations flow from changes in attitude towards the fundamental sources of Islam, the Qur'an and the *sunna*, although, in most instances, the abstract intellectual discussions regarding these sources are not brought to the forefront when Muslims conceptualize their basic religious practices within the modern context. What continues to be of interest for our purposes, however, is the way in which the issues and approaches employed in the considerations of the Qur'an and the *sunna* are also manifested in the approaches to the various issues which surround the role and function of ritual practice in the contemporary context.

THE PILLARS OF ISLAM

The traditional definitional elements of Muslim faith – the summaries of belief and the ritual 'five pillars' – remain virtually intact in the modern context. Any movement towards prayers being said in the vernacular rather than Arabic, for example, or towards being able to perform the fast for the month of Ramadan in a more 'convenient' month, has proven singularly unsuccessful. But this should not be taken to suggest that the modern world has not had an impact on Muslim practice at all. Attention to Islamic ritual activities and their practice provides a means of looking at ways Muslims have attempted to express their religiosity in general; within the modern context, several factors lead to these ritual aspects of Islam having a significant bearing on the question of the contemporary manifestation of Islam.

What might be termed the politicization of Muslims, a world-wide phenomenon in Islam but especially prevalent in diaspora populations in North America and Europe, has led to a heightened sense of identity being felt through the affirmation of distinctive Islamic practices. Another way of expressing this is as 'the Islamization of the self', and the use of Islamic symbols to provide identity on a personal level.[1] This tendency is connected with the move of individuals not only from a rural to an urban society but also, one might contend, from a 'Muslim' society to a 'non-Muslim' one. Village society has always been characterized by the idea that 'the life of the village is the religion of the village'; that is, the rhythm of life reflects the Islamic way and is integral to each member's life. Modern society, especially that of a predominantly non-Muslim country, displays a separation between religious life and secular life which has led to a tendency towards affirming various aspects of Muslim existence – notably those associated with ritual activity and self-study of the Qur'an – as central tenets of identity. Identity in these cases is a personal one, not a collectively affirmed one as in the community-based village life. The observations made in the previous chapter regarding the idea of veiling, *hijab*, being a personal, home-focused idea serve as an additional example of this reorientation. Such personalization of faith is frequently a core element of fundamentalism, it may be remarked.[2]

This tendency towards personalization of faith may be the result of the general globalization of Islam within the world community. While Islam certainly spread widely in previous centuries, the present-day mobility of world populations along with massive dislocations of various groups within many countries has had some significant consequences. The status of Muslim minorities around the world has become an issue for Muslims, not perhaps impinging upon their self-definition within Islam in the same way as the creation of a diaspora-centred Judaism did, but significant nevertheless, and it may well have an even greater impact in the future.[3]

Islam has always defined itself ritually as being focused on the 'five pillars'. In connection with each ritual, the impact of the modern world may be noted, not so much in the practices themselves necessarily but in the interpretation which is put forth of the activities. It is, therefore, not a matter of continuing to legitimate the activities themselves in the modern context but a question of how to mould them to the modern age within an Islamic framework and how to conceptualize them in relation to ideas of self-definition. It is this principle which displays, in a very practical sense, the ramifications of the approaches towards reinterpretation of the Qur'an and the *sunna*, as discussed earlier in this book.

WITNESS TO FAITH (*SHAHADA*)

The *shahada*, or 'witness to faith', is the first of the classical 'five pillars' of Islam. Repeating the sentence, 'I witness that there is no god but God and I witness that Muhammad is the messenger of God' in Arabic, preceded by a statement of intention (as are all rituals in Islam), provides an entry into the community of Islam for any individual. The statement of the *shahada* is also repeated as an integral part of the Muslim prayer and gains its full ritual status in that context. An example of the contextualization of the *shahada* in contemporary American society is provided by the following statement within a wedding ceremony, addressed to the bride who intended to convert to Islam:

> 'There is no priesthood in Islam. Anyone can perform the [wedding] ceremony, even you yourselves, or a trusted representative of the bride and groom. I do not like the term *conversion*. Sister, you are not converting, you are reforming. Islam is not only the religion of Muhammad, it is also the religion of Moses and Jesus. The term *Christianity* was not used by Jesus but only by later generations, who modified his teachings. Thus, when we say, "There is only one religion and that is Islam," we mean that all the prophets carried the same message from the same God. Sister, you are not obliged to convert to Islam. You may keep your religion intact if you wish to do so.' Sue indicates her need to 'reform'. Nasem says, 'Then let it be so.' He explains the three foundations of Islam: oneness of God, prophethood, and resurrection. . . .
>
> Then come the two testimonies: 'Sister, repeat after me, I witness there is no God but God, Muhammad is His servant slave and His messenger.' Then prayer: all present raise their hands and pray that she might be a good Muslim and have a happy, prosperous life. Then the marriage ceremony.[4]

Radical Islamists have often attempted to define Islam in terms of the witness to faith alone, by emphasizing the concept of *tawhid*, the oneness and unity of God, as expressed in the *shahada*. This follows from a statement made by Muhammad as reported within the *hadith* material to the effect that he brought nothing more important than the *shahada*. The idea of *tawhid*, then, for the Radical Islamists, expresses everything which Islam stands for and is the basis of all Islamic thought; such a summary is a crucial part of the suggestion that Islam is a 'simple' religion, in that once the truth of this affirmation of the oneness of God is perceived, then everything else in Islam flows from it.

So, when you recite these words [of the *shahada*], you should be conscious what an important commitment you are making to your God, with the whole world as your witness, and what a great responsibility you are taking on as a result of your commitment. Once you have made the affirmation consciously, the Kalimah [literally 'the word', meaning the words of the *shahada*] must inform all your thoughts and reign supreme in your whole lives: no idea contrary to it should form part of your mental furniture. Whatever runs counter to the Kalimah you must always consider false and the Kalimah alone true. . . .

If you recite the Kalimah in this manner, only then can you become true Muslims, only then is created that overwhelming difference between man and man.[5]

The statement of the *shahada*, then, is the essence of the Radical Islamist totalism in the vision of Islam.

PRAYER (*SALAT*)

Five specific periods of prayer a day are a ritual requirement in Islam. Spread throughout the day and into the night at set times, prayer consists of a set pattern of recitations and bodily movements repeated a set number of times. It is performed in a ritually purified state while facing in the direction of the Ka'ba in Mecca. Recitation of sections of the Qur'an is an integral part of the prayer. Friday is the day of communal prayer when all male members are required to gather at the mosque at noon.

The globalization of the Muslim population has created a number of incongruous situations illustrating the way in which Islam has been confronted with the realities of the modern context.[6] In Surinam, Indians, brought by the Dutch to that country in the period 1873–1916 (by 1982, there were 50,000 such people), are Hanafis in their legal school alignment. They conduct their sermon (*khutba*) during the Friday noon prayer in Urdu and they face the east (their *qibla*) during all the prayer. The Javanese present in Surinam, on the other hand, are Shafi'is according to their legal school and have a *qibla* to the west. These people were indentured labourers brought by the Dutch in the period 1850–1931, and by 1982 there were 90,000 of them. 'The *qibla* is towards the west simply because it is in this direction in Java, although Mecca is situated from Surinam in the easterly direction', according to Rolf Reichert, who researched this issue. This is, of course, not a 'problem' for Islam in any sense; that any group of people would continue to follow their traditional direction of prayer in any given place does not impinge upon significant elements of Muslim self-definition. It does indicate, however, that as the process of globalization continues, such elements may continue to grow and may well provoke questioning on the part of Muslims themselves.

A similar, and likewise essentially trivial, element is presented by Muslims flying in outer space and locating the direction of prayer and the time of prayer; this latter point also applies to those in polar regions where timings as related to the sun's position will provide suitable intervals for prayer. In most such situations, people agree that the timings of prayer in Mecca should be followed. The point here is that the modern context provokes a situation in which the fundamental principles of ritual activity in Islam must be faced. The solutions are argued on a legal basis, employing well-established juristic principles, extrapolated for the required situation.

More substantial issues related to prayer most certainly do exist and they reflect the extent to which Muslims have been willing to adapt ritual to the social context in which they live.

The implementation of Sunday as the day of congregational prayer (*juma'*) rather than Friday has been one such issue. In 1935, Atatürk made Sunday the weekly day of closing for offices, factories and so forth in Turkey. Such a 'day of rest' had not been instituted during the pre-industrial age of Islamic society and had never been seen as a religiously based necessity (the Qur'an suggests that the sabbath as a day of rest was a special legal provision for the Jews). Atatürk's action was justified by him in terms of practical concern for life in the modern age.[7] Such a step did not, however, transform Muslim worship with its focus on Friday noon for communal prayer. In other countries, however, especially those with Muslim groups living within a primarily Christian context, the move to Sunday became an entire transformation of the Muslim day of communal gathering. Like similar movements within Reform Judaism which tried sabbath worship on Sundays rather than Saturdays within the context of European (Christian) society, this was a relatively short-lived accommodation to the society around them. For Muslims, Friday was (re-)asserted to be the day which was attached to a very basic sense of Islamic identity. What still remains in more contemporary times is the use of Sunday as a 'family day' with mosque-centred activities (for example, 'Sunday school' as religious training for children).

For the performance of the Friday communal prayer, a prayer leader, *imam*, is required; his function is to lead the community in prayer, keeping the actions in unison, and he will frequently (but not always) be called upon to deliver the *khutba* or sermon. This has raised another issue related to the wide dispersal of Muslims today in countries where they are not the majority of the population. In many instances, an *imam* is recruited from outside the country. This is often done as a way of helping to maintain the identity of the minorities, but in some situations this only emphasizes the foreignness of a minority group. Furthermore, these imported *imam*s are often felt to be out of touch with the realities of life in the new countries in which they are living.

Malise Ruthven has pointed this out as a factor in acerbating the 'Rushdie affair' in England. The arrival of the *imams*, in this case brought in from Pakistan to Bradford, reinforced

> the ties with the homeland, creating an anchor with the certainties of the past. It also reinforces isolation: few of the *imams* know English; fewer still are aware of the wider British society around them with its complexities and diversified spiritual resources. The leaders add spiritual authority to a vision of society already viewed, one might say distorted, through the prism of faith: the society that corresponds to the *jahiliyya* of the Prophet's time, a godless, materialistic society wholly dedicated to the pursuit of worldly wealth and sensual pleasure.[8]

Equally significant in this regard, however, is the extent to which these prayer leaders have been thrust into adopting a general ministerial role, something essentially foreign to the nature of the office in the past and also in predominantly Muslim countries today. A new institution has essentially arisen within the North American and European context for Muslims.[9]

Overall, the interpretation of prayer in modern Muslim discussions has often taken on a certain spiritualized interpretation. Rarely is prayer presented as simply a duty to be fulfilled because it has been decreed by God. Rather, prayer is described as the primary defence of the Muslim against the encroachment of worldly concerns, for 'it prevents an individual from all sorts of abominations and vices by providing him chances of direct communion with God'.[10] The present spiritual leader of Iran, Ayatullah 'Ali Khamenei, is reported to have suggested the following:

> no other channel is a better means for communicating with the Almighty, and . . . a 'Salat' said with full cognizance of its deeper meanings and with a full heart is the best safeguard for man against a tendency to succumb to a feeling of absurdity and moral weakness.[11]

FASTING (*SIYAM, SAWM*)

Abstention from all food and drink as well as avoidance of sexual intercourse during daylight hours is the mark of the Muslim thirty-day period of fasting, carried out during the month of Ramadan, the ninth month of the Muslim lunar calendar.

Ramadan has always been considered by most Muslims as the most important of the ritual duties. Even if a person does not comply with the requirement of five prayers a day, observance of the fast is still likely. Contemporary Muslim fast participants do, however, exhibit subtle changes in the interpretation of their actions. While in earlier times a sense of the penitent value of fasting was certainly present, this has been downplayed in the interpretations of recent decades. The fast is performed because it has been commanded by God, not for any individual benefit which may accrue to the individual in terms of his or her fate in the hereafter. Moral benefit in the here and now, however, is emphasized. The fast is a means of social levelling and of reinforcing notions of social responsibility. When even the rich are hungry, the fate of the poor will be evident, so the argument goes. Even more, there is an overall sense of Muslim unity celebrated during the fast, especially in the festive aspects of nightlife during the month.

Various attempts have been made, especially under government impetus, to modify this area of Muslim practice. President Bourguiba of Tunisia, in February of 1960, for example, urged the avoidance of Ramadan observances for government employees.[12] Religion should serve to ameliorate life, not make it more difficult, his argument went; in the present state of Tunisia's attempts to thrive as an independent country, fasting would only worsen the economic condition and the suffering which would result from the month of fasting was a type of penitence foreign to Islam. Certain religious scholars supported this stance on the grounds that *jihad*, 'holy war', was needed in order to build the country economically, and fasting for those fighting in times of *jihad* was not necessary according to Islamic law.[13] Similar suggestions were reported in Egypt in the mid-1950s.[14] These 'reforms', however, based upon an impetus towards greater efficiency in (capitalist) society, proved extremely unpopular, even among those who did not partake in the fasting. Those who argued against changing the requirements of Ramadan said that the legislation imposed by God could not be changed by the opinion of a lowly human being. Fasting, according to the argument against change, is intimately tied to hardship; that is the essence of it, indeed. ('Where is the fasting person who does not suffer hardship in fasting?', it was asked.) Just because economic hardship might result from fasting did not give a reason not to fast; if it did, then nobody would bother to fast, everyone claiming that it involved hardship.[15] In fact, the whole logic of fasting was to provide the experience of hardship for those who might otherwise never have it. The argument for the rationality of Islamic ritual is notable. Overall, these types of argument and the tide of public sentiment led governments to a compromise position of restricting working hours in government offices and factories during the month.

It has been pointed out by some observers that the concern which Muslims expressed over this issue of Ramadan observance was far more severe than that expressed regarding many other changes which were taking place in the Muslim world at that time. Polygamy, for example, was banned in several countries during this period. The issue, therefore, was perceived to be one not of changing the law, as such, but of an attack on Muslim identity:

Ramadan had become in modern times the great manifestation of the unity of Islam, the month when Muslims believing or unbelieving became conscious of their past and affirmed their links with their ancestors, and the criticism [of the practice of Ramadan] was perhaps resented not because it ran counter to the *Shari'a* but rather because it threatened the solidarity of the Muslim community.[16]

Fasting has continued to be a significant element in Muslim identity up to today, and that status has been emphasized within the context of the often-noted assertiveness of Muslim minority groups in minority situations. One interesting instance of this contemporary politicization of Muslims may be illustrated through an incident at my own university. During the spring of 1991, the final examination period for students fell during Ramadan. This, of course, is not the first time this would have happened in recent times, with Ramadan moving eleven days forward from one solar calendar year to the next. However, in this particular year, the Administration experienced an apparently new phenomenon: requests for 'deferred final examinations' from Muslims on the grounds of the religious requirement of fasting during daylight hours which would, reasonably enough it was argued, make undertaking an examination difficult. It is the focus on Ramadan that is significant. North American society, after all, ignores all aspects of the Muslim ritual calendar. Students have not demanded that classes should not take place during prayer times (not even Fridays) nor that those wishing to go on pilgrimage to Mecca be excused from any academic responsibilities. (Christmas and Easter remain central to the academic schedule, however.) Ramadan is an individual religious action which is particularly amenable to the general North American religious ethos; the assertion of its prominence in the ritual calendar, therefore, is a part of the contextualization of the Muslim community in the modern world.

Determining when Ramadan should start and the precise hours of fasting on any given day has been accommodated to modern technology and order. Traditionally, the religious calendar has been established each month through the siting of the moon.[17] Observing the hours of fasting for Muslims living in polar regions has raised issues, therefore, as for prayer times. Once again, a pragmatic solution is brought forth. But for some people, this is an argument about science and tradition. Science can now tell us with great accuracy when the month of Ramadan starts and ends. Back in Muhammad's time, the only practical means of determining the month was by observation of the moon. It only makes sense (and God urges such in the Qur'an), so the argument goes, that today Muslims should embrace the scientific accuracy which is available.

The traditional practice of the recitation of the Qur'an during the nights of Ramadan continues, celebrating the revelation of the Qur'an to Muhammad during that month. Modern media participate in the event with radio stations playing Qur'an recitation. Even in officially secular Turkey, the publication of the appropriate one-thirtieth section of the Qur'an in Turkish (Roman) characters each day in the newspaper was undertaken during the 1980s.

CHARITY (*ZAKAT, SADAQA*)

The giving of alms (*zakat*) has been, within the juridical system of classical Islam, a fully regulated system. Depending on the source of the income and its size, anywhere between $2\frac{1}{2}$ and 20 per cent of amounts in excess of certain stipulated limits is to be given to various classes of recipient.

Modern terminology and principles have been applied to *zakat*, especially in countries outside the Muslim heartlands where the economic systems presuppose, if not demand, certain forms of financial participation. Thus we see '*Zakat* Returns' just like 'Income Tax Returns', where statements of net worth are subject to calculation of the tax owing. Such 'Returns' often present an uneasy compromise between the realities of modern Euro-American life and the traditional categories of items on which *zakat* is collectable; they may also feature certain aspects which might not be seen as being fully in keeping with a system of 'Islamic economics' as that proposed, and partially enacted, by some Radical Islamists (such as taking into account interest paid on mortgages and loans).

Similar problems with the payment of *zakat* must be faced in the more central Islamic lands also. Is *zakat* to be paid on types of property unknown in classical Islamic times? Just what do stock certificates represent? Should the tax be paid in stock certificates or in cash? At what percentage? Likewise there is the issue of who should receive the *zakat*, with the traditional list – the poor, new converts, travellers, missionaries, those who collect the tax, slaves (for buying their freedom) and those who have debts due to public service – frequently being extended to include modern charitable institutions.[18] Such issues are generally solved through the processes of Islamic law, such as reasoning by analogy, but the significant fact, of course, is that the issue does have to be faced.[19]

Zakat and politics have mixed extensively in Pakistan where charity and income tax have often been equated; it has been argued that only the modern state apparatus can actually handle the equitable distribution of these funds, given the complexities of modern life.[20] Likewise, *zakat* and the idea of egalitarianism as fitting in with the socialist platforms were especially prominent under Nasser in the Egypt of the 1960s.[21] Islamic charity is equated to a system of responsibility fundamental to Islamic social structures and social assumptions. The sharing of wealth legitimizes one's own possession of material goods and emphasizes the communal aspects of ownership in Islam.[22]

Finally, another way of solving the entire problem of how *zakat* is to be understood in the modern world has arisen. There has been a tendency to remove *zakat* altogether from its juridical context and simply make it free-will offerings. This is one more aspect of the emergence of a personalized and individualized Islam, common among the Radical Islamist group. But this exists in tension with ideas of Islamic economics in which the only legitimated system of taxation (and taxation would seem essential to the modern nation-state, Islamic or otherwise) is that of *zakat*. It is also argued that *zakat* must be given in the proportions which have been established in the *sunna*, regardless of whether they are needed or not; the basis of a taxation system, however, is that the amount 'given' varies with the needs of the government. Fundamentally, it is an issue of whether or not charity is to be viewed as a purificatory rite for the devout: if so, then the demands of a government to extract it subvert that sense of offering which seems essential to such a view. Could Muslims ever consider a compulsory tax which is assessed and deducted from one's pay cheque as a religious offering?[23] At the same time, the sense of the communal nature of Islam and the legitim-ation of the political aspects of the religion through the model of Muhammad leads more frequently to an assertion of the state's responsibility for collection of the tax. This would appear to be the motivation behind a recent (1991) suggestion in Malaysia that the government should legislate for the giving of *zakat*, with penalties of up to three years in jail, an $1800 fine and six strokes of the cane for non-payment. Even the threat of such legislation would seem to be having an effect, according to authorities who have seen a 75 per cent rise in contributions to the Islamic Treasury in 1991 compared to 1990.[24]

PILGRIMAGE (*HAJJ*)

Lasting up to seven days, the ritual of the pilgrimage focuses upon Mecca and its environs and is enjoined for performance at least once in a lifetime for all Muslims who are physically and financially able to come to the city, male or female. Undertaken during the first half of the last month of the year, Dhu'l-Hijja, the pilgrimage requires the pilgrim to be in a state of ritual purity and to don the pilgrimage clothes before its activities are undertaken and before entering the area of Mecca. Once the preparations have been completed by the pilgrim, the Ka'ba is circumambulated and a run is performed between al-Safa and al-Marwa, two hillocks near the Ka'ba, joined to the Meccan mosque by a covered arcade; this is usually done on the 4th of Dhu'l-Hijja. Both activities are performed seven times, interspersed with prayers and invocations. On the 7th day of the month, the actual pilgrimage starts with a ritual purification and a prayer service at the mosque around the Ka'ba. On the next day (the 8th), the pilgrims assemble in Mina, just outside Mecca, and most stay there for the night although some go on to 'Arafat. The next morning (the 9th) the pilgrims assemble near the plain of 'Arafat, 15 kilometres east, on the Mount of Mercy, where a prayer ritual is performed and a ceremony called the 'standing' is undertaken, lasting from the time the sun passes the meridian until sunset. That evening, the pilgrims return to Muzdalifa, about half-way back to Mina, where the night is spent. The next day (the 10th) a journey to Mina brings them to the stone pillar, at which seven stones are thrown, in a ritual understood to represent the repudiation of Satan. This is followed by a ritual slaughter of sheep, goats and camels and a meal, the *'id al-adha*, the 'festival of the sacrifice', which is performed by all Muslims whether on the pilgrimage or not. Returning to Mecca, the Ka'ba is circumambulated and the running between al-Safa and al-Marwa (unless completed before the pilgrimage) is performed. The state of ritual purity is abandoned on this day, symbolized by the men having their heads shaved and women having a lock of hair cut off. Three days of celebration at Mina follow for most pilgrims, with more stones thrown at three pillars of Satan and followed by another circumambulation of the Ka'ba. A visit to Medina is also often included before the pilgrims return home.[25]

The pilgrimage presents ritual, legal, social, administrative, symbolic and ethical aspects, all of which have a particular and distinctive flavour in the modern period.

There is a tendency in apologetic works towards rationalism in aspects of pilgrimage ritual. Regarding the black stone lodged in the side of the Ka'ba which pilgrims attempt to touch while circumambulating the shrine, for example, a symbolic status alone is often attributed to it; any connection of the stone to pre-Islamic times and to stone worship, as was classically affirmed by Muslim writers, will be ignored. The stone is just a natural stone from Mecca, according to Mahmud Shaltut of Egypt. Such interpretations exist in tension, however, with those which emphasize the power of the stone and thus affirm its pre-Islamic significance.[26] Such issues have arisen primarily because of the confrontation of modern historical questioning and traditional religious conceptions. Some aspects relate to 'irrational' matters: is the black stone really a rock descended from heaven as was held in the past? How could that possibly be?

More generally, according to one study of contemporary popular religious literature, there is a marked reluctance on the part of many writers to acknowledge any continuation of pre-Islamic practices within Islamic rituals such as the pilgrimage. The 'Islamization' of pagan rituals is ignored, for it is felt, apparently, that such historical research may well be destructive to Islam, even though observations about these connections were widespread in classical Islam. The preferred view today is to see all elements of Islam as having been revealed by God, sometimes even to the point of ignoring the idea that there had ever even been a pre-Islamic pilgrimage. Interestingly, Sayyid Qutb provides a contrary view:

> In these verses [of the Qur'an] we see how Islam turned the [*hajj*] into an Islamic commandment, removed its pagan roots and made it into one of the supporting pillars of Islam, adorned it with Islamic notions and cleansed it from its blemishes and dregs . . . , indeed, this is the way of Islam with every custom and ceremony which it deemed right to maintain.[27]

The most popular way of understanding all the pilgrimage rituals is to emphasize their symbolic and spiritual value: throwing stones at the pillars represents not the external Satan but the internal Satan in the individual's heart. In general, the acts of the pilgrimage may appear 'irrational' but their performance provides a way for the individual to show devotion to God; interpretation or relating the elements to their historical symbolic referents is unnecessary, if not undesirable, therefore. The pilgrimage is portrayed as an event in which the power and grandeur of God may be experienced by all Muslims, regardless of their origin or social status.[28] In some of the more imaginative symbolic interpretations, such as that of 'Ali Shari'ati, various aspects of the *hajj* become symbols of Islamic life: the *sa'y*, which in its historical interpretation is the running back and forth in search of water of Hagar, becomes 'activism', the struggle of life in the world for what is needed in daily living and the struggle against economic and political oppression. *Tawaf*, the circumambulation of the Ka'ba, is symbolic of 'endeavour', especially in the striving towards a correct, divinely oriented life of devotion.[29]

Beyond the interpretation of the activities of the pilgrimage, there are substantial issues related to the level of participation. The Saudi Arabian government has provided the following statistics for *hajj* visitors from foreign countries (numbers for Saudi resident participation are available only through estimations):

1982	853,555
1983	1,003,911
1984	919,671
1985	851,761
1986	856,718
1987	960,386

In 1989, the total number was 774,560, comprising 460,250 males and

314,310 females.[30] The drop in number, compared to 1987, may be explained by the absence of pilgrims from Iran (who, in 1987, numbered 157,395). Behind this, then, is another modern issue for Islam, one which vexes Muslims tremendously. The pilgrimage, a ritual required for all Muslims who are able, takes place not solely on a personal level but also as a ritual which is undertaken in a modern nation-state, Saudi Arabia. It is, therefore, both under the control of that state and also that state's responsibility. In 1987, over 400 pilgrims, mainly Iranians, were killed during violent demonstrations. As a result, the Saudi government cut ties with Iran and limited the number of Iranian pilgrims to 45,000. Iran retaliated by refusing to allow participation in the *hajj* at all. This situation lasted until 1991, when Iranians once again joined in; estimates for that year's total pilgrimage participation were put at 2 million.[31] Regulations concerning how often foreign residents of Saudi Arabia may perform the pilgrimage are another method instituted by the government to control attendance. The idea that participation in a fundamental ritual of the religion should be controlled by a given political regime has created substantial difficulties for some Muslims; calls for the internationalization of Mecca are sometimes voiced as a result. The political aspects of the issue – the alliances between Saudi Arabia and the United States being a focal point of many allegations – result in the pilgrimage frequently becoming a symbolic element in the struggle between modern nations. Ayatullah Khumayni of Iran, for example, described the pilgrimage as the most important time for Muslims to demonstrate their unity and their rejection of imperialism:

What is the solution, and what is the responsibility of the Muslims and oppressed for dispelling these illusions [of their powerlessness]? The primary solution, from which emerges all other solutions for cutting the roots of these problems and eradicating corruption, is the unity of Muslims, rather the unity of all oppressed and enslaved peoples in the world. This unity is gained through widespread *tabligh* [missionizing] and invitation. And the centre for this invitation and *tabligh* is the holy city of Makkah [Mecca] during the congregation of Muslims to perform the Hajj. This was started by Ibrahim, continued by Muhammad and will be followed by Hadrat Mahdi [who, the Shi'ites believe, will return at the end of time]. It was enjoined on Ibrahim to call people to Hajj to attend to their needs – that is, the political, social, economic and cultural issues of the society – and so that they, could witness how God's Prophet laid upon the altar the fruit of his life, for the sake of God. . . .

We renounce the infidels during the Hajj rituals. This is a political-religious renunciation that the Prophet Muhammad, upon whom be peace, enjoined.[32]

On top of the question of political control of access, other implications also arise as a result of modern conveniences allowing participation in the pilgrimage. Most pilgrims now fly directly to Jedda in Saudi Arabia before commencing on their way to Mecca. (In 1989, 534,662 foreign pilgrims arrived by air, 43,948 by sea and 195,950 by land.) The number of pilgrims handled in Saudi Arabia has increased tremendously (in 1869, some 110,000 foreigners participated; in 1907, 250,000)[33] but the implications of this are felt all over the Muslim world, especially in the social significance which results from participation in the pilgrimage. Richard Antoun reports that in the Jordanian village which he studied, a general rise in annual income (resulting from working in the Saudi Arabian oil industry), modern, safe and rapid transportation methods and government encouragement of local pilgrim guides had all resulted in a marked rise in the proportion of the inhabitants who had performed the pilgrimage between the years 1959 and 1986.[34] This was accompanied, however, by a change in the ethos related to pilgrimage performance. It used to be the case, according to Antoun, that pilgrimage brought both status within the community and the requirement for the pilgrim of appropriately pious behaviour; it was, therefore, something which was reserved for the older men of the community who, it was felt, would be able to carry the burden of that responsibility. Today, a far greater proportion of younger men (under 40 and generally well educated) undertake the pilgrimage as a means of asserting religious identity.

Flying to Jedda to commence the pilgrimage has some direct ritual implications. Traditionally, the state of purity represented by the clothing known as the *ihram* (along with other associated rituals) would be donned before entering the region of the *mawaqit* or boundaries of the sacred area, within which Jedda sits. Pilgrims coming by air, therefore, as a rule put their pilgrimage costume on in their home country before boarding the plane, although it is considered possible to do it in Jedda.[35] Certain other aspects of the rituals are now likely to be spread over a number of days rather than all the pilgrims being able to accomplish them all at once. The very crush of people has required an extra storey to be built at the mosque of Mecca, something which is considered in legal terms an innovation yet one which was necessary. Some people have urged that the pilgrimage be stretched over a longer period of time so that everyone may be accommodated. Substitutions for the animal slaughter which is an integral part of the activity have been suggested, so that a person should need to give up (i.e. sacrifice) something 'held dear', just as Abraham was willing to give up his son, the action which the sacrifice recalls.[36] As it stands, the sacrifices have become centralized. In 1987 and 1988, pilgrims bought coupons from al-Rajhi Company for Currency Exchange and Commerce, which sold them on behalf of the Islamic Development Bank's Sacrificial Meat Utilization

Project. A sheep (of which some 600,000 are imported, mainly from Australia) is then slaughtered on behalf of the pilgrim in a modern abattoir according to prescribed Muslim ritual slaughtering methods. The meat is quick frozen and later distributed to refugee populations around the Muslim world.[37] Modern issues of hygiene clearly dictate that 600,000 animals could not be slaughtered in the outdoor environs of Mecca. Such hygienic concerns are also raised in relationship to the housing and facilitating of the massive influx of pilgrims themselves.

ISLAMIC SYMBOLS AND SOCIAL IDENTITY

In modern Muslim life much attention is given to the attempt to implement Islamic ideals in society in general: this may be summarized generally as the impact of Islam upon politics. This is to be associated primarily with the Islamic totalist vision, in which the idea that Islam 'encompasses all of life' has become the central pivot for political aspirations. Religion also becomes a political tool in this framework, as in the frequent charge that Islam is used by many political leaders simply to justify change and keep the masses quiet. Here it is a matter of the social use of Islamic symbols rather than the personal use of them.[38] It is here too where we realize that Islam as a faith in the modern world has two faces: the personal, ever-searching and flexible, and the institutional, firm and imperialistic.[39]

The interpretation of Islamic ritual activity illustrates the tension which would seem to be present in some of the conceptualizations of Islam today. Bringing the personal and the institutional together in a rapidly moving world of conflicting interests seems beyond most discussions. Those which attempt such a feat often take on an air of unreality, as, for example, in the discussion of Islamic economics. Underlying them all are the basic motifs already noticed in discussions of the place of Muhammad and the Qur'an: anti-supernaturalism, an accommodation with science, a debate over legal provisions versus moral imperatives. The presentations of ritual often seem to be on the defensive, viewing the activities as the final barrier of the individual against modernity. It is not surprising, then, that for many Muslims, the rituals assume a place as the keystone of their self-identity as Muslims. It should not be forgotten, however, that for many Muslims this resurgence or added emphasis on ritual is a feature only of those alienated from their Islamic roots anyway. The integration of Muslim life in the more rural parts of the Muslim world continues as it ever has and may well do in the same manner for many generations to come.

Conclusions: contemporary Muslim religiosity

PUTTING MATTERS IN PERSPECTIVE

In this book we have looked at the vigorous discussions which Muslims have undertaken in modern times over topics related to the status and interpretation of the fundamental religious sources of authority. As well, we have seen how some of these ideas have had ramifications in social and ritual life. But just what all this might mean in terms of Muslim religiosity is a question which still must be faced. The question is not easy to approach, however. Richard Antoun puts it well:

> How are we to determine, for instance, whether the building of new mosques, the establishment of government-sponsored religious publishing houses, the setting aside of special places in parliament for prayer, the establishment of religious political parties, or the establishment of bureaus to safeguard the Holy Quran are indications of religious-mindedness, indications of a shift in the attitudes of elites only, or simply an increase in political action in the name of Islam? Is an increasing use of Arabic, an increase in veiling, an increase in attendance at the Friday congregational prayer, or an increase in pilgrimage to be taken as an increase in piety, religious-mindedness, or hypocrisy?[1]

The fact is that the range of contemporary Muslim religiosity varies tremendously. One of the reasons for this is that people understand and 'use' religion in a variety of ways; that is true whether we are dealing with Islam or Christianity or any other religion. The following summary within a recent anthropological study provides an interesting perception of the ways in which Islam manifests itself:

> In this village, Islam can take the form of a bland legalism or a consuming devotion to the good of others; an ideology legitimizing established status and power or a critical theology challenging this very status and power; a devotive quietism or fervent zealotism; a dynamic political activism or

self-absorbed mysticism; a virtuoso religiosity or humble trust in God's compassion; a rigid fundamentalism or reformist modernism; a ritualism steeped in folklore and magic or a scriptural purism.[2]

The basis for these variations appears to depend on a wide variety of factors: childhood experiences, individual personality, education, general social context and so forth. All the variations, however, emphasize the independence of thought which is possible even within a society frequently characterized by its apparent uniformity. Plainly, Islam is a multi-faceted phenomenon which is able to encompass within its fold many different views of the world and of religion in general.

This list of variations in religious practice is useful for stimulating two further thoughts; they may serve to place the discussions into which this book has delved in their proper perspective. Both are issues which deserve extensive treatment in their own right, but for our purposes here, it is sufficient just to broach them. There are two points to make here: one, we must remember that devotion to the learning of the past continues to live in conjunction with interaction with the pressures of the contemporary world. By no means are all aspects of Muslim religiosity mired in debate. Two, and not totally separate from the previous reminder, we must note the role of the mystical trend in Islam known as Sufism and its place in the lived religion.

CELEBRATING MUHAMMAD'S BIRTHDAY

Brief attention to the celebrations connected with the birthday of Muhammad may help to clarify these issues. Known generally as *mawlid al-nabi*, 'the birth of the prophet', the celebration of this day does not have an official status in Islam; that is, this commemoration of the day is not recorded in the classical texts of Islamic law and has no connection to the *sunna*. When jurists did contemplate it in later centuries, they often termed it a *bid'a hasana*, a commendable innovation. Historically, the present festival is thought to stem from the twelfth century; this is when the historians of the period start to record various practices related to the twelfth day of the month of Rabi' I, which was designated as Muhammad's birthday. The activities within the celebration are characteristic of the general Muslim approach towards honouring local saints. *Mawlid*s were, and still are, held for the most popular holy men and women of Islamic history as a part of mystical devotion. A holy day emerges from its connection with a holy person, a day on which celebrations and devotions may be expected to bring great merits and benefits. The central events of such days are processions (frequently lit with candles or the like), chanting, singing and telling stories. A fair is often organized for the children. The celebrations culminate in religious devotions to the holy person, producing 'exaltation, fervor, rapture and in many a tranquil contentment'.[3] Today, in most of the Muslim world, the birthday of Muhammad is celebrated in a similar manner. Each area has its own particular form of celebration and in many countries it has become an official state holiday. This official character is reinforced by the presence of the head of state, who will frequently attend the festivities held at the main mosque in the capital city.[4]

Characteristic of the celebration is the recitation of poetry in praise of Muhammad, often known as *mawladiyya*. Much of the material found in the poems recited today is derived from classical sources,[5] which emphasize the observation above concerning the continued role of and devotion to the learning of the past. Despite many people's consciousness of the existence of more 'modern' biographies – those that downplay Muhammad's miracles and emphasize his human qualities as previously explored – the image of Muhammad as portrayed in the older works continues to be a vital piece of the practised faith.

As well, the characteristics of the poetry reveal a definite mystical element which has permeated Muslim belief. One example of the Sufi influence may be seen in the theory espoused in much of the poetry regarding the pre-existent 'Muhammadan Light', an element of the miraculous but also the salvific nature of the conception of Muhammad through which this world is connected to the divine domain. A typical poem contains the following lines:

> The lights of Muhammad streamed upon us,
> The full moons have hurried away; we have never seen such beauty.
> Only you are the face of happiness.
> You are a sun; you are a full moon.
> You are light upon light.
> You are an elixir, very precious
> You light up [our] hearts, my Beloved Muhammad.
> You are the bride of both East and West
> You are firmly backed [by God] and honored,
> You are the Imam of the the two qiblas.
> Whoever gazed upon your face felt elated.
> You are from distinguished parentage and your background is peerless.[6]

Along with the recitation of poetry in honour of Muhammad on these occasions, a more definitive element of Sufi practice creeps in. The poetry is often followed by a *dhikr*, the repetition of mystical litanies often formed around the name of God. This will not always be the case on the actual day of the celebration of Muhammad's birthday but frequently occurs on other occasions on which the person of Muhammad is invoked for blessing, such as in marriages. The performance of the *mawlid* poetry becomes the task of entertainers hired for the purpose. The poetry is not limited to praise of Muhammad, but that theme always 'brackets the proceedings'.[7]

Reactions against the *mawlid*

The entire celebration of the *mawlid*, whether connected to Muhammad or to specific Sufi saints (the latter celebration often referred to by a variety of names), frequently raises the ire of Muslims who wish to 'purify' Islam of all elements that cannot be explicitly supported by the regulations of the Qur'an or the practice of Muhammad. This attitude is often one which is also the most suspicious of past learning, seeing the scholars of earlier times as having made things too difficult.

However, the power of Sufism, both in its institutionalized form and in the way that its general influence is felt in Islam as a whole, suggests that this Fundamentalist vision of Islam certainly does not represent anywhere near a majority of Muslims. Recent anthropological studies especially have shown that, throughout the Muslim world, Sufi brotherhoods remain a vital part of the religious environment.[8] The desire for an emotional aspect to religious life, in combination with the appeal of images which glorify Muhammad and, indeed, the divine, has a substantial place in Islam and this is frequently provided by the Sufi tradition. Grouped around a spiritual leader and following certain practices designed to stimulate the experience of God, Sufi brotherhoods flourish throughout the Muslim world, even if they are not always condoned by governments or establishment religious forces.

MUSLIM RELIGIOSITY

Muslim faith is a complex phenomenon, just as is any other religion. It may be tempting to suggest that there are two different faces to Muslim religiosity: the intellectual debate over principles of the faith confronting the personal practice of individual Muslims. The danger here is that we may exaggerate a dichotomy which, while it may have a certain analytical convenience, may lead to a distortion of the presentation of Muslim faith. Better would be a conception which sees faith on a continuum, attempting self-conscious definition at times and reaching into the experiential dimension of religion in order to refresh those definitions at other times. This would seem to be the genius of religion, and of Islam especially.

Glossary

adab 'morals' or 'courtesy'; the habitual way of acting in accordance with social standards.

Allah Arabic for God.

amir commander or prince, frequently used in reference to the person who leads the community.

Ash'arites followers of the theological school named after al-Ash'ari (d. 935).

dhimmi a member of a protected community, especially referring to the Jews and Christians who live under Muslim rule. The right to practise their own religion was guaranteed by their payment of a special poll tax, the *jizya*.

din religion; the word is used in the Qur'an to refer to the specific beliefs and practices of people.

fatwa a legal decision rendered by a *mufti*, who is a jurist qualified to make decisions of a general religious nature.

fiqh jurisprudence, the science of religious law, as described by the jurists known as the *fuqaha'*.

hadith a tradition or written report, being the source material for the *sunna* of Muhammad, gathered together in the six books of authoritative traditions in Sunni Islam.

hajj pilgrimage to Mecca performed in the month of Dhu'l-hijja, one of the 'five pillars' of Islam; a requirement for all Muslims, if they are able, once in a lifetime.

Hanbalites followers of the Sunni school of law named after Ahmad ibn Hanbal (d. 855).

hijab the veil or partition which prevents men from gazing at the 'charms of women'. A variety of styles exist but most emphasize covering the hair and hiding the shape of the body.

hijra Muhammad's emigration from Mecca to Medina in the year

622CE, understood as the date for the beginning of the Muslim *hijri* calendar.

ihram   the state of consecration into which the pilgrim enters (thus becoming a *muhrim*) in order to perform the *hajj* or the *'umra*.

i'jaz   a doctrine which states that the Qur'an cannot be imitated; the 'inimitability' of the Qur'an.

ijma'   'consensus', one of the four sources of law in Sunni Islam, the others being Qur'an, *sunna* and *qiyas*.

ijtihad   the use of one's 'personal effort' in order to make a decision on a point of law not explicitly covered by the Qur'an or the *sunna*; the person with the authority to do this is called a *mujtahid*.

imam   literally the 'model', here generally referring to the prayer leader in the *salat* who stands in front of the rows of worshippers, keeping their actions in unison during the prayer. The word is also used in other contexts. It is a title of the revered early leaders of the Shi'ites who are the source of authority in that community; these imams are 'Ali ibn abi Talib and certain of his descendants who were designated as holding the position. The word is also commonly used as a title of the founders of the Sunni schools of law – Abu Hanifa, Malik ibn Anas, al-Shafi'i and Ibn Hanbal – and similarly for other significant religious figures.

islah   'reformism', especially in the nineteenth-century Arab world as proposed by people such as Muhammad 'Abduh.

isma'   a doctrine which states that the prophets, and especially Muhammad, were protected from sin (*ma'sum*) during their lifetimes. It is also applied to the Shi'ite Imams.

isnad   the chain of authorities through whom a *hadith* report has passed; the list of these people forms the first part of the *hadith* report, the text which comes after it being called the *matn*.

isra'   Muhammad's 'night journey' to Jerusalem, connected to the heavenly ascension, *mi'raj*.

jahiliyya   the 'Age of Ignorance', historically seen to be before Muhammad but in a general religious sense referring to ignoring, or ignorance of, Islam; especially used with moral overtones.

jihad   'striving for the faith' or 'holy war', sometimes seen as a 'sixth pillar' of Islam.

jinn   'sprites' or genies, another dimension of animate creation on earth.

juma'   in reference to prayer, *salat*; it is the Friday noon gathering of the community which is enjoined in the Qur'an and which takes place in the *jami'* or congregational mosque.

Ka'ba   the sacred black cube building in the middle of the mosque in Mecca; Muslims face in the direction of the Ka'ba when they perform the ritual prayer (*salat*) and circumambulate it when they perform the pilgrimage (*hajj* or *'umra*).

khalifa   Caliph, the leader of the Sunni community, the 'successor' to Muhammad.

madhhab   a school of law formed around one of the four early figures significant in juristic discussions (Abu Hanifa, Malik ibn Anas, al-Shafi'i, Ibn Hanbal); plural: *madhahib*.

matn   the text of a *hadith* report, as compared to the *isnad*, the chain of transmission.

mawlid   birthday; specifically the celebration of the birthday of Muhammad.

mi'raj   the 'heavenly ascension' of Muhammad, reported to have taken place around the year 6 of the *hijra*, in which he met with the prophets of the past, was given visions of heaven and hell, gazed upon God and was given the command of five prayers a day for all Muslims.

mufti   a jurist who is authorized to give a *fatwa* or legal decision on a religious matter.

mujaddid   a renewer of the faith, stated in a *hadith* report to appear in the Muslim community every 100 years, in order to revive the true spirit of Islam through the process of *tajdid*, 'renewal'.

mujtahid   a jurist who is qualified to exercise *ijtihad* or personal effort in making legal decisions on matters where there is no explicit text of the Qur'an or the *sunna* to be followed.

Mu'tazila   a theological school of thought which blossomed in the eighth and ninth centuries; it stressed human free will and the unity and justice of God, and embraced Greek rationalist modes of argumentation. In modern times, certain thinkers (e.g. Muhammad 'Abduh) are sometimes considered neo-Mu'tazilites because of their reintroduction of some of these ideas.

muwaqit   the locations at which the pilgrim's *ihram* clothing is put on for the performance of the pilgrimage (*hajj*).

nahda   the renaissance of the Muslim world in general that was pictured by reformers as resulting from the cultural renewal which would take place in modern times.

purdah   a term from India referring to seclusion and veiling of women; the same as *hijab*.

qadi	a judge who makes decisions on the basis of the religious law.
qibla	the direction which one faces in prayer (Mecca), marked by the *mihrab* in the mosque.
qiyas	'analogy', one of the four sources of law in Sunni Islam, the others being Qur'an, *sunna* and *ijma'*.
salat	the prescribed five prayers a day, one of the 'five pillars' required of all Muslims.
sawm	fasting performed in the month of Ramadan, one of the 'five pillars' required of all Muslims (also called *siyam*).
Shafi'ites	followers of the school of law named after al-Shafi'i (d. 820).
shahada	'witness to faith'; saying (in Arabic), 'There is no god but God and Muhammad is His messenger'; one of the 'five pillars' required of all Muslims, indicating conversion to Islam but also a part of the ritual prayer (*salat*).
shari'a	the religious law derived from the four sources of law in Sunni Islam (Qur'an, *sunna*, *qiyas* and *ijma'*).
Shi'ites	the religio-political party championing the claims of 'Ali ibn abi Talib and his heirs to the rightful leadership of the community and to their status as imams; since the beginning of the sixteenth century, Shi'ism has been the official state religion of Iran and most of its followers live there. They comprise about 10 per cent of the world population of Muslims.
Sira	the biography of Muhammad as found in written form.
Sufi	an adherent of the mystical way of Islam, Sufism, *tasawwuf*.
sunna	'custom'; the way Muhammad acted which is then emulated by Muslims. The source material for the *sunna* is found in the *hadith* reports. The *sunna* is one of the four sources of law for Sunni Islam, along with Qur'an, *qiyas* and *ijma'*.
Sunnis	the majority form of Islam, those who follow the *sunna* (thus being called the *ahl al-sunna*), who do not recognize the authority of the Shi'ite Imams.
sura	a chapter of the Qur'an.
tafsir	interpretation of the Qur'an, especially as found in written form. Such books generally follow the order of the Qur'anic text and pay attention to the meaning of each word or sentence.
taqlid	the reliance upon decisions made in the past in matters of religious law; the word is set in opposition to *ijtihad*, 'personal effort', and frequently has a negative sense in the modern context.
tasawwuf	Sufism, the mystical way in Islam.
tawhid	doctrine holding to the proclamation of the unity of God.
'ulama'	the learned class, especially those learned in religious matters.

umma	the community; the body of Muslims.
'umra	the 'visitation' of the holy places in Mecca, the lesser pilgrimage; it can be performed at any time of the year but is also joined with the *hajj*.
Wahhabi	the followers of Ibn 'Abd al-Wahhab (d. 1787); a revivalist-purificatory movement in Arabia which became (and continues to be) the official religious policy of Saudi Arabia.
zakat	alms tax, one of the 'five pillars' required of all Muslims.

Notes

INTRODUCTION

1 M.G.S. Hodgson, *The Venture of Islam. Conscience and History in a World Civilization*, vol. 3: *The Gunpowder Empires and Modern Times*, Chicago, IL, University of Chicago Press, 1974, p. 216.

2 H.A.R. Gibb, *Modern Trends in Islam*, Chicago, IL, University of Chicago Press, 1947, p. viii.

3 Kenneth Cragg, 'Religious Developments in Islam in the 20th Century', *Cahiers d' histoire mondiale/Journal of World History*, 3 (1956), 505.

4 One of the best and most readable reflections on the problems involved here is to be found in Hodgson, op. cit., pp. 175–205.

1 DESCRIBING THE CONTEMPORARY WORLD

1 Fazlur Rahman, *Islam*, 2nd edition, Chicago, IL, University of Chicago Press, 1979, p. 214.

2 Harvey Cox, *Religion in the Secular City: Toward a Postmodern Theology*, New York, Simon and Schuster, 1984, p. 182.

3 See David Lowenthal, *The Past is a Foreign Country*, Cambridge, Cambridge University Press, 1985, for illustrations of a variety of aspects of this.

4 In his *Facing up to Modernity: Excursions in Society, Politics, and Religion*, New York, Basic Books, 1977, pp. 70–80.

5 See Cox, op. cit., p. 183.

6 See R.J. Zwi Werblowsky, *Beyond Tradition and Modernity: Changing Religions in a Changing World*, London, The Athlone Press, 1976, p. 11.

7 See ibid., pp. 23–6.

8 See Edward Said, *Orientalism*, New York, Pantheon Books, 1978.

9 See, for example, W.M. Watt, *Islamic Fundamentalism and Modernity*, London, Routledge, 1988, and my review of that book in *Journal of Semitic Studies*, 36 (1991), 367–9.

10 Cited from an unnamed source in Emmanuel Sivan, *Radical Islam: Medieval Theology and Modern Politics*, New Haven, CT, Yale University Press, 1985, p. 11.

11 In her *Contemporary Islam and the Challenge of History*, Albany, NY, State University of New York Press, 1982, pp. 13–23.

12 See John J. Donohue, 'Islam and the Search for Identity in the Arab World', in

John L. Esposito, ed., *Voices of Resurgent Islam*, New York, Oxford University Press, 1983, pp. 48–61.

13 See Fouad Ajami, *The Arab Predicament: Arab Political Thought and Practice since 1967*, Cambridge, Cambridge University Press, 1981, for some views (many quite controversial) on the impact of the 1967 Arab– Israeli war and the 1973 oil boycott.

14 See Bruce B. Lawrence, *Defenders of God: The Fundamentalist Revolt against the Modern Age*, San Francisco, CA, Harper and Row, 1989, p. 195, who refers to this with the nice formulation, 'the mythologization of oil'.

15 Op. cit., p. 11.

16 A biting social critique of this aspect of modern Arab life is presented in the 1989 Algerian/French film *De Hollywood à Tamanrasset*, directed by Mahmoud Zemmouri.

17 Allan Bloom, *The Closing of the American Mind*, New York, Simon and Schuster, 1987, pp. 69, 73, 74. The American public's self-flagellation in making a best-seller of this work must be understood as a part of the general ambivalence felt by many towards the modern period.

18 Clifford Geertz, *Islam Observed. Religious Development in Morocco and Indonesia*, New Haven, CT, Yale University Press, 1968, p. 3.

19 See, for example, the discussion of these concepts in Mohammed Arkoun, *Rethinking Islam Today*, Washington, DC, Center for Contemporary Arab Studies, Georgetown University, 1987, pp. 13–14.

20 Seyyid Hossein Nasr, 'The Shari'ah and Changing Historical Conditions', in his *Islamic Life and Thought*, Albany, NY, State University of New York Press, 1981, pp. 27–30.

21 Werblowsky, op. cit., p. 19.

22 See Cox, op. cit., p. 186.

23 Ibid., pp. 186–7.

24 Note that, given the context of the publication of this essay, its likely audience was conceived to be people without the ability to read the Qur'an in Arabic, i.e. non-Muslims and Muslims without formal religious training.

25 Mark C. Taylor, *Erring. A Postmodern A/theology*, Chicago, IL, University of Chicago Press, 1984, p. 3.

26 The concept of the *imaginaire*, not really captured by the English 'imagination', is central to Arkoun's thought. See the discussion in Arkoun, op. cit., esp. pp. 20–3.

27 They are frequently disposed of by English speakers as incomprehensible.

2 ISLAM'S ENCOUNTER WITH THE CONTEMPORARY WORLD

1 The terms 'normative', 'neo-normative' and 'acculturating' are used in Yvonne Y. Haddad, *Contemporary Islam and the Challenge of History*, Albany, NY, State University of New York Press, 1982, pp. 7–12. See also William E. Shepard, 'Islam and Ideology: Towards a Typology', *International Journal of Middle East Studies*, 19 (1987), 327–8, note 2, for a full review of other terms and categories used in various analyses. It may also be observed that this kind of separation makes some sense in comparative religion terms if the separations are seen in terms of both authority of the past and attitude to change: Judaism's

division between Orthodox, Conservative and Reform and even Christianity's Catholic, Evangelical and Protestant may all be analysed in these terms. The history of the development of these groups makes the situation of each religion quite different, however.

2 See John Esposito, 'Tradition and Modernization in Islam', in Charles Wei-hsun Fu and Gerhard E. Spiegler, eds, *Movements and Issues in World Religions. A Sourcebook and Analysis of Developments since 1945. Religion, Ideology, and Politics*, New York, Greenwood Press, 1987, p. 96.

3 W. Montgomery Watt, *Islamic Fundamentalism and Modernity*, London, Routledge, 1988, Ch. 1, argues that this position is inherent in Islam because of its view of religion as unchanging, linked to the notion of the eternal word of God, etc. He also sees this as a reflection of ancient bedouin notions of the world which are fully ingrained in the Islamic ethos. This seems highly doubtful.

4 See Fazlur Rahman, 'Islam: Challenges and Opportunities', in Alford T. Welch and Pierre Cachia, eds, *Islam: Past Influence and Present Challenge*, Edinburgh, Edinburgh University Press, 1979, pp. 317–18.

5 Fazlur Rahman, 'Internal Religious Developments in the Present Century Islam', *Cahiers d' histoire mondiale/Journal of World History*, 2 (1955), 863–4.

6 For this point in its overall context see Yvonne Haddad, 'Muslim Revivalist Thought in the Arab World', *The Muslim World*, 76 (1986), 143–67; for more details see also John O. Voll, 'Renewal and Reform in Islamic History: *Tajdid* and *Islah*', in John L. Esposito, *Voices of Resurgent Islam*, New York, Oxford University Press, 1983, pp. 32–47.

7 Fazlur Rahman, 'Islam: Challenges and Opportunities', op. cit., p. 317.

8 For a sample of his writing see Andrew Rippin and Jan Knappert, eds, *Textual Sources for the Study of Islam*, Manchester, Manchester University Press, 1986 (reprinted Chicago, IL, University of Chicago Press, 1990), Section 9.3.

9 For a sample of his writing see ibid., Section 9.2.

10 For a sample of his writing see ibid., Section 9.1.

11 See *Encyclopaedia of Islam, New Edition*, 'islah' (by Ali Merad).

12 Ibid.; see also Ali Merad, 'Reformism in Modern Islam', *Cultures*, 4 (1977), 108–27.

13 For more on the Ahmadiyya see Antonio R. Gualtieri, *Conscience and Coercion. Ahmadi Muslims and Orthodoxy in Pakistan*, Montreal, QC, Guernica, 1989; Yohannan Friedmann, *Prophecy Continuous. Aspects of Ahmadi Religious Thought and its Medieval Background*, Berkeley, CA, University of California Press, 1989. For samples of Ahmadi writings see Rippin and Knappert, op. cit., Section 7.4.

14 For samples of Baha'i writings see Rippin and Knappert, op. cit., Section 7.3.1–4.

15 See Bruce Lawrence, *Defenders of God: The Fundamentalist Revolt against the Modern Age*, San Francisco, CA, Harper and Row, 1989, p. 79: 'Ideology is motivational to this world, not cognizant or reflective of the other world. It is on this point that the content of ideology and religion diverge most widely. Religions are marked by rites of passage for the individual, while ideologies aim to mobilize energies towards achieving corporate goals.' Lawrence's whole discussion of ideology, especially pp. 76–80, is worthy of close attention.

16 See Shepard, op. cit.; this article is also a mine of bibliography on the subject of modern Islam in general.

17 Ibid., p. 313.

18 Ibid., p. 313.
19 ' "Fundamentalism" Christian and Islamic', *Religion*, 17 (1987), 355–78; see also his 'What is "Islamic fundamentalism"?', *Studies in Religion*, 17 (1988), 5–26.
20 See Shepard, ' "Fundamentalism" Christian and Islamic', op. cit., and the critiques of it by Bruce Lawrence and Azim Nanji, *Religion*, 19 (1989), 275–84.
21 Lawrence, *Defenders of God, passim*, e.g. p. 201.
22 See Rahman, 'Islam: Challenges and Opportunities', op. cit., pp. 315–19. On this point, compare the analysis of Bruce B. Lawrence, 'Muslim Fundamentalist Movements: Reflections toward a New Approach', in Barbara Freyer Stowasser, ed., *The Islamic Impulse*, London, Croom Helm, 1987, pp. 15–36.
23 For some samples of Imam Khumayni's popular writings (reflecting the ideology of the revolution) see Rippin and Knappert, op. cit., Sections 9.4.1 and 9.4.2.
24 Edward Said, *Orientalism*, New York, Pantheon Books, 1978; also his *Covering Islam. How the Media and the Experts Determine How We See the Rest of the World*, New York, Pantheon Books, 1981. The impact of these books on contemporary Western scholarship will form an interesting piece of research; see Emmanuel Sivan, *Interpretations of Islam, Past and Present*, Princeton, NJ, Darwin Press, 1985, Ch. 5, on the Arab reaction to Said's work, but see also my review of Sivan's book, *Bulletin of the School of Oriental and African Studies*, 51 (1988), 329–30.
25 See the review by Mohammed Arkoun of Y.Y. Haddad, B. Haines and E. Findly, eds, *The Islamic Impact*, in *Arabica*, 32 (1985), 106, for this point.
26 Shabbir Akhtar, *A Faith for all Seasons. Islam and Western Modernity*, London, Bellew, 1990.
27 Ibid., p. 84.
28 Malise Ruthven, *A Satanic Affair. Salman Rushdie and the Rage of Islam*, London, Chatto and Windus, 1990, p. 128, questions Akhtar regarding the status of women as indicated in the Qur'an: that a woman's testimony is worth half that of a man's, Akhtar said, is 'a scandal of faith. . . . God decrees what He pleases. We have to accept it, that's the scandal of faith. God's commands sometimes seem impossible: but we are duty-bound to obey.'
29 Ibid., p. 129. Ruthven did not have the benefit of reading Akhtar's book when writing this work; his remarks are extremely perceptive.

3 MUHAMMAD AND HIS BIOGRAPHERS

1 See James E. Royster, 'Muhammad as Teacher and Exemplar', *The Muslim World*, 68 (1978), 235–56, although note that not all of his sources are from the contemporary period.
2 For a summary of various modern views on this aspect of Muhammad's biography see Jamel Eddine Bencheikh, *Le voyage nocturne de Mahomet*, Paris, Imprimerie Nationale, 1988, pp. 251–7.
3 For an overview of the topic see Annemarie Schimmel, *And Muhammad is His Messenger: The Veneration of the Prophet in Islamic Piety*, Chapel Hill, NC, University of North Carolina Press, 1985, especially the last two chapters; the work also has an excellent bibliography.
4 Muhammad Husayn Haykal, *The Life of Muhammad* (trans. Isma'il Ragi A. al Faruqi), Indianapolis, IN, North American Trust Publications, 1976, pp. 579–80.

5 See Charles D. Smith, *Islam and the Search for Social Order in Modern Egypt: A Biography of Muhammad Husayn Haykal*, Albany, NY, State University of New York Press, 1983, pp. 113–25.

6 Haykal, op. cit., pp. 184–5.

7 Quoted in Charles C. Adams, *Islam and Modernism in Egypt. A Study of the Modern Reform Movement Inaugurated by Muhammad 'Abduh*, London, Oxford University Press, 1933, pp. 256–8, from Taha Husayn, *Al-Adab al-Jahili*, 2nd edition, 1927.

8 M.G.S. Hodgson, *The Venture of Islam. Conscience and History in a World Civilization*, vol. 3: *The Gunpowder Empires and Modern Times*, Chicago, IL, University of Chicago Press, 1974, p. 294.

9 Antonie Wessels, *A Modern Arabic Biography of Muhammad. A Critical Study of Muhammad Husayn Haykal's Hayat Muhammad*, Leiden, E.J. Brill, 1972, p. 9. For an excellent treatment of Taha Husayn and other writers on Muhammad in the context of creative literature, see M.M. Badawi, 'Islam in Modern Egyptian Literature', in his *Modern Arabic Literature and the West*, London, Ithaca Press, 1985, esp. pp. 58–60.

10 See Earle H. Waugh, 'The Popular Muhammad', in Richard C. Martin, ed., *Approaches to Islam in Religious Studies*, Tucson, AZ, University of Arizona Press, 1985, p. 54.

11 Jacques Jomier, 'Une vie de Mohammad, apôtre de la liberté', *Mélanges d'institut dominicain d'études orientales du Caire*, 8 (1964–6), 395–400; also Wessels, op. cit., pp. 19–24; Badawi, op. cit., 61–3.

12 'Abd al-Rahman 'Azzam, *The Eternal Message of Muhammad*, New York, Devin-Adair, 1964; Mentor Books, 1965, pp. 204–5.

13 Ibid., pp. 141–2.

14 An example of this is Martin Lings, *Muhammad: His Life Based on the Earliest Sources*, London, George Allen and Unwin, 1983.

15 Kenneth Cragg, *The Pen and the Faith. Eight Modern Muslim Writers and the Qur'an*, London, George Allen and Unwin, 1985, p. 159. It should be noted that some have argued against this sort of interpretation of Mahfouz's work, but such tendencies seem to aim more towards saving Mahfouz from charges of blasphemy than towards appreciation of the literary merits of the work; as an example, see Jareer Abu-Haidar, 'Awlad Haratina by Najib Mahfuz: An Event in the Arab World', *Journal of Arabic Literature*, 16 (1985), 119–31.

16 Wessels, op. cit., pp. 24–9.

17 See Malise Ruthven in *The (London) Times Literary Supplement*, 25 November–1 December 1988, p. 1312.

18 Cragg, op. cit., pp. 157–8.

19 Issa J. Boullata, *Trends and Issues in Contemporary Arab Thought*, Albany, NY, State University of New York Press, 1990, p. 132.

20 Fatima Mernissi, *Beyond the Veil. Male–Female Dynamics in Modern Muslim Society*, revised edition, Bloomington, IN, Indiana University Press, 1987, p. 9.

21 Fatima Mernissi, *Women and Islam: An Historical and Theological Enquiry*, Oxford, Basil Blackwell, 1991, p. 104. This is the translation of Mernissi's French work *Le harem politique: le prophète et les femmes*, Paris, A. Michel, 1987, which has been published in the United States under the title: *The Veil and the Male Elite: A Feminist Interpretation of Women's Rights in Islam*, Reading, MA, Addison-Wesley, 1991.

22 Ibid., pp. 163–4.

23 Ibid., p. 185.
24 'Ali Dashti, *Twenty-three Years: A Study of the Prophetic Career of Mohammad* (trans. F.R.C. Bagley), London, George Allen and Unwin, 1985, p. 158; also see my review of this book in *Bulletin of the School of Oriental and African Studies*, 50 (1987), 547–8.
25 Dashti, op. cit., p. 208.
26 Ibid., p. 137.
27 See Andrew Rippin and Jan Knappert, eds, *Textual Sources for the Study of Islam*, Manchester, Manchester University Press, 1986 (reprinted Chicago, IL, University of Chicago Press, 1990), Sections 7.1.2 and 7.1.3 for a version of the traditional story relating to Husayn. On Khumayni's use of Shi'ite symbols in general see Mangol Bayat, 'The Iranian Revolution of 1978–79: Fundamentalist or Modern?', *Middle East Journal*, 37 (1983), 30–42.
28 Shaykh Muhammad Mahdi Shams al-Din, *The Rising of al-Husayn. Its Impact on the Consciousness of Muslim Society* (trans. I.K.A. Howard), London, Muhammadi Trust, 1985, p. xiii. This foreword is signed 'The Muhammadi Trust'. This book was one in a series planned to consist of four titles written in the 1970s by Muhammad Mahdi Shams al-Din on Imam Husayn.
29 Ibid., p. 23.

4 THE AUTHORITY OF THE PAST

1 Aslam Jairajpuri, teacher of Ghulam Ahmad Parvez, as cited in J.M.S. Baljon, 'Pakistani Views of Hadith', *Die Welt des Islams*, NS 5 (1958), 225.
2 Abu Dawud, *Sunan*, Beirut, al-Maktaba al-Asiya, 1980, vol. 4, pp. 197–8; English translation by Ahmad Hasan, *Sunan Abu Dawud: English Translation with Explanatory Notes*, Lahore, Sh. Muhammad Ashraf, 1984, vol. 3, p. 1290.
3 al-Bukhari, *al-Sahih* (bilingual Arabic–English edition, trans. Muhammad Muhsin Khan), Chicago, IL, 3rd edition, Kazi Publications, 1977, vol. 3, p. 373.
4 Muslim ibn al-Hajjaj, *Sahih Muslim*, Beirut, Mu'assasat 'Izz al-Din, 1987, vol. 1, p. 34. An English translation of this work is available: Abdul Hameed Siddique, *Sahih Muslim*, Lahore, M. Ashraf, 1971.
5 Sheila McDonough, *The Authority of the Past. A Study of Three Muslim Modernists*, Chambersburg, PA, American Academy of Religion, 1970, p. 1, speaks of this as an 'articulated legitimization'.
6 Ibid., p. 3.
7 Aziz Ahmad, *Islamic Modernism in India and Pakistan 1857–1964*, London, Oxford University Press, 1967, p. 37.
8 McDonough, op. cit., p 12.
9 Ahmad, op. cit., p. 50.
10 McDonough, op. cit., p. 14.
11 See R.A. Butler, 'Ghulam Ahmad Parvez: Ideological Revolution through the Qur'an', *Al-Mushir*, 17 (1975), 1–37.
12 G.A. Parvez, *Islam: A Challenge to Religion*, Lahore, Idara-e-Tulu-e-Islam, 1968, provides a good introduction to his general thought as connected with the Qur'an.
13 J.M.S. Baljon, *Modern Muslim Koran Interpretation (1880–1960)*, Leiden, E.J. Brill, 1961, pp. 17–19; also Baljon, 'Pakistani Views of Hadith', op. cit., pp. 219–27.

14 Muslim ibn al-Hajjaj, op. cit., vol. 5, p. 500. See the treatment of the discussion of this point in Egypt in G.H.A. Juynboll, *The Authenticity of the Tradition Literature. Discussions in Modern Egypt*, Leiden, E.J. Brill, 1969, Ch. 5.

15 See Andrew Rippin, *Muslims: Their Religious Beliefs and Practices*; vol. 1: *The Formative Period*, London, Routledge, 1990, Chs 2 and 3, although the motivation in the past appears to have been conservatism – the 'fear of innovation' – as compared to today's 'rejection of innovation in the past' as pointed out by Baljon, 'Pakistani Views of Hadith', op. cit., p. 227; but this may really only indicate the relativeness of all such terms.

16 Quoted in Baljon, 'Pakistani Views of Hadith', op. cit., p. 224, from Parvez's *Maqam-i Hadith*.

17 Fazlur Rahman, 'Internal Religious Developments in the Present Century Islam', *Cahiers d' histoire mondiale/Journal of World History*, 2 (1955), 873.

18 Charles J. Adams, 'The Ideology of Mawlana Mawdudi', in Donald Eugene Smith, ed., *South Asian Politics and Religion*, Princeton, NJ, Princeton University Press, 1966, pp. 371–97; Adams, 'Mawdudi and the Islamic State', in John L. Esposito, ed., *Voices of Resurgent Islam*, New York, Oxford University Press, 1983, pp. 99–133; Kurshid Ahmad and Zafar Ishaq Ansari, 'Mawlana Sayyid Abul A'la Mawdudi: An Introduction to his Vision of Islam and Islamic Revival', in their edited volume, *Islamic Perspectives. Studies in Honour of Mawlana Sayyid Abul A 'la Mawdudi*, Jedda, Saudi Publishing House; Leicester, The Islamic Foundation, 1979, pp. 359–83.

19 See Elizabeth Sirriyeh, 'Modern Muslim Interpretations of *Shirk*', *Religion*, 20 (1990), 139–59 (esp. 149–51).

20 Baljon, 'Pakistani Views of Hadith', op. cit., p. 225.

21 Ibid., pp. 225–6. For the polemic in the other direction – Mawdudi against Parvez – see Maryam Jameelah, 'Islam minus Sunnah: A Critical Review of the Work of Ghulam Ahmad Parvez', in her *Islam and Modernism*, Lahore, Mohammad Yusuf Khan, 1975, pp. 97–104.

22 Charles J. Adams, 'The Authority of the Prophetic Hadith in the Eyes of Some Modern Muslims', in Donald P. Little, ed., *Essays on Islamic Civilization presented to Niyazi Berkes*, Leiden, E.J. Brill, 1976, p. 35.

23 See the magazine *Arabia* (London), October 1986, pp. 36–7.

24 Judith Nagata, *The Reflowering of Malaysian Islam. Modern Religious Radicals and their Roots*, Vancouver, BC, University of British Columbia Press, 1984, p. 217.

25 The forthcoming study by Howard Federspeil, *Strengthening Behavior: Hadith Usage in Contemporary Indonesia*, suggests a limited impact of this tendency towards radical questioning of the *sunna* in Southeast Asia. The political dimensions of the Malaysian case may have to be seen as more determinative, therefore.

26 See Charles C. Adams, *Islam and Modernism in Egypt. A Study of the Modern Reform Movement Inaugurated by Muhammad 'Abduh*, London, Oxford University Press, 1933, pp. 173–5.

27 A fine example of this is found in the medical traditions examined in Juynboll, op. cit., Ch. 11.

5 TRENDS IN INTERPRETATION

1 Cf. John B. Henderson, *Scripture, Canon and Commentary. A Comparison of Confucian and Western Exegesis*, Princeton, NJ, Princeton University Press, 1991, p. 221: 'The abandonment or supersession of commentarial forms in the intellectual culture of early-modern times has often gone unremarked. Yet this development is probably of greater significance in the intellectual transition between the medieval and modern worlds than most of the great ideas of leading philosophers and scientists of this same age. For the form of the commentary influenced modes of thought, and did not just provide the format for their expression.'

2 Fazlur Rahman, 'Internal Religious Developments in the Present Century Islam', *Cahiers d' histoire mondiale/Journal of World History*, 2 (1955), 872.

3 On 'Abduh, see Charles C. Adams, *Islam and Modernism in Egypt. A Study of the Modern Reform Movement Inaugurated by Muhammad 'Abduh*, London, Oxford University Press, 1933; also H.A.R. Gibb, *Modern Trends in Islam*, Chicago, IL, University of Chicago Press, 1947, Chs 2 and 3.

4 See Muhammad 'Abduh, *The Theology of Unity* (trans. Ishaq Musa'ad and Kenneth Cragg), London, George Allen and Unwin, 1966.

5 See Jacques Jomier, *Le commentaire coranique du Manar. Tendances modernes de l' exégèse coranique en Egypte*, Paris, Maisonneuve, 1954. In more recent times, Mahmud Shaltut, head of al-Azhar University in Cairo 1958–63, has continued with this type of moderate modernism in the context of Qur'an interpretation; see Kate Zebiri, 'Shaykh Mahmud Shaltut: Between Tradition and Modernity', *Journal of Islamic Studies*, 2 (1991), 210–24.

6 Helmut Gatje, *The Qur' an and its Exegesis: Selected Texts with Classical and Modern Muslim Interpretations*, Berkeley, CA, University of California Press, 1976, p. 249.

7 Azad as cited in I.H. Azad Faruqi, *The Targuman al-Qur' an; A Critical Analysis of Mawlana Abu' l-Kalam Azad's Approach to the Understanding of the Qur' an*, New Delhi, Vikas Publishing, 1982, p. 73.

8 Ashfaque Husain, *The Quintessence of Islam. A Summary of the Commentary of Maulana Abul Kalam Azad on al-Fateha, the First Chapter of the Quran*, Bombay, Asia Publishing House, 1960, pp. 68, 69 (originally published in 1958 under the title *The Spirit of Islam*).

9 An excellent presentation of the core ideas is found in Yvonne Yazbeck Haddad, 'The Qur'anic Justification for an Islamic Revolution: The View of Sayyid Qutb', *The Middle East Journal*, 37 (1983), 14–29; also see her 'Sayyid Qutb, Ideologue of the Islamic Revival', in John Esposito, ed., *Voices of Resurgent Islam*, New York, Oxford University Press, 1983, pp. 67–98.

10 Sayyid Qutb, *Fi' l-Ta' rikh: Fikra wa-Minhaj*, as quoted in Yvonne Y. Haddad, *Contemporary Islam and the Challenge of History*, Albany, NY, State University of New York Press, 1982, p. 90.

11 These are, of course, the ideals claimed for the Western liberal, democratic tradition, but Qutb emphasizes the absolute sovereignty of God within a truly Islamic society; see Leonard Binder, *Islamic Liberalism: A Critique of Development Ideologies*, Chicago, IL, University of Chicago Press, 1988, Ch. 5.

12 Sayyid Qutb, *In the Shade of the Qur' an* (trans. M. Adil Saladi and Ashur A. Shamis), London, MWH London Publishers, 1979, vol. 30, p. 249.

13 See Emmanuel Sivan, *Radical Islam: Medieval Theology and Modern Politics*,

New Haven, CT, Yale University Press, 1985, Ch. 2.

14 A.H. Johns, 'Let my People Go! Sayyid Qutb and the Vocation of Moses', *Islam and Christian–Muslim Relations*, 1 (1990), 143–70.

15 See Binder, op. cit., pp. 190ff in reference to Sayyid Qutb's work *al-Taswir al-Fanni fi' l-Qur'an*; also see Johns, op. cit., p. 148, and Issa J. Boullata, 'The Rhetorical Interpretation of the Qur'an: *I'jaz* and Related Topics', in Andrew Rippin, ed., *Approaches to the History of the Inter- pretation of the Qur'an*, Oxford, Oxford University Press, 1988, pp. 150–1.

16 An interesting account of her biography is available in C. Kooij, 'Bint al-Shati': a Suitable Case for Biography?', in I.A. el-Sheikh, C.A. van de Koppel and R. Peters, eds, *The Challenge of the Middle East. Middle Eastern Studies at the University of Amsterdam*, Amsterdam, University of Amsterdam, 1982, pp. 67–72.

17 See Issa J. Boullata, 'Modern Qur'an Exegesis: A Study of Bint al-Shati''s Method', *The Muslim World*, 64 (1974), 103–13. Also see Kenneth Cragg, *The Mind of the Qur'an. Chapters in Reflection*, London, George Allen and Unwin, 1973, pp. 70–4.

18 Further insights are to be found in William M. Brinner, 'An Egyptian Anti-Orientalist', in G. Warburg and U.M. Kupferschmidt, eds, *Islam, Nationalism, and Radicalism in Egypt and the Sudan*, New York, Praeger, 1983, pp. 228–48.

19 See J. Jomier, 'Le Cheikh Tantawi Jawhari (1862–1940) et son commentaire du Coran', *Mélanges de l' institut dominicain d' études orientales du Caire*, 5 (1958), 115–74.

20 Haluk Nurbaki, *Verses from the Glorious Koran and the Facts of Science (V)* (trans. Metin Beynam), Ankara, Turkish Foundation for Religious Publications, 1986, p. 44. There are many other examples of such books in English; see, for example, Ghulam Sarwar, *Philosophy of the Quran*, Lahore, Muhammad Ashraf, 1938.

21 This statement comes from an interview with Khaled aly Khaled in a side-bar called 'Living Islam' in Mary Pat Fisher and Robert Luyster, *Living Religions*, Englewood Cliffs, NJ, Prentice-Hall, 1991, p. 277.

22 See also J. Jomier, 'L'exégèse scientifique du Coran d'après le Cheikh Amin al-Khouli', *Mélanges de l' institut dominicain d' études orientales du Caire*, 4 (1957), 269–80.

23 Shabbir Akhtar, *A Faith for All Seasons. Islam and Western Modernity*, London, Bellew, 1990, p. 54.

24 See Ali Merad, *Ibn Badis, commentateur du Coran*, Paris, Librairie Orientaliste Paul Geuthner, 1971.

25 See his *The Quran in Islam. Its Impact and Influence on the Life of Muslims* (trans. Assadullah ad-Dhaakir Yate), London, Zahra Publications, 1987; also S.H. Nasr, H. Dabashi and S. Vali Reza Nasr, eds, *Shi'ism: Doctrines, Thought and Spirituality*, Albany, NY, State University of New York Press, 1988, Ch. 3, on Tabataba'i and another contemporary Iranian thinker, Mutahhari.

26 See A.H. Johns, 'Quranic Exegesis in the Malay World: In Search of a Profile', in Rippin, ed., op. cit., pp. 275–8. For contemporary, printed *tafsirs*, see Howard M. Federspiel, 'An Introduction to Qur'anic Commentaries in Contemporary Southeast Asia', *The Muslim World*, 81 (1991), 149–65, and Federspiel, *Popular Indonesian Literature of the Qur'an*, Ithaca, NY, Modern Indonesia Project, 1992.

6 TYPES OF CRITICAL APPROACHES

1 The translations of the following three passages are from Abdullah Yusuf Ali, *The Holy Qur-an*, Beirut, Dar al-Arabia, 1968 (but many prints exist); the translation is accompanied by an extensive commentary in the footnotes in which it exhibits Modernist tendencies (especially in its desire to 'spiritualize' various aspects) which are also reflected in the translation itself.

2 As, for example, in the Ahmadi translation by Maulawi Sher Ali.

3 *Asia Week*, 27 April 1990, p. 37, a side-bar to an article entitled 'A New Morality for India'.

4 Shabbir Akhtar, *A Faith for All Seasons. Islam and Western Modernity*, London, Bellew, 1990, Ch. 3, also argues against the traditional assessment of the Qur'an in terms of its form – an argument which has no persuasive value among opponents, he says – and prefers the argument from results. He does not use this as a basis for questioning the non-contingent nature of the text (which he maintains) but simply as a more effective argument.

5 See, for example, Fazlur Rahman, *Major Themes of the Qur'an*, Minneapolis, MN, Bibliotheca Islamica, 1980, p. 98.

6 Edgar Krentz, *The Historical Critical Method*, Philadelphia, PA, Fortress Press, 1975, p. 19.

7 Ibid., p. 24.

8 Ibid., p. 33, quoting and translating Ulrich Wilckens, 'Über die Bedeutung historischer Kritik in der modernen Bibelexegese', in *Was heisst Auslegung der Heiligen Schrift?*, Regensburg, Friedrich Pustet, 1966, p. 133.

9 Arthur Jeffery, 'The Suppressed Commentary of Muhammad Abu Zaid', *Der Islam*, 20 (1932), 303.

10 See Jacques Jomier, 'Quelques positions actuelles de l'exégèse coranique en Egypte révélées par une polémique récente (1947–1951)', *Mélanges d'institut dominicain d'études orientales du Caire*, 1 (1954), 39–72, in connection with the Arabic translation of the *Encyclopaedia of Islam* article on *tafsir* by al-Khawli.

11 See Yvonne Y. Haddad, *Contemporary Islam and the Challenge of History*, Albany, NY, State University of New York Press, 1982, pp. 46–53; see also Haddad's article, 'Islamic "Awakening" in Egypt', *Arab Studies Quarterly*, 9 (1987), 241, for observations on Khalaf Allah's present political role in presenting the religious plank of a left-leaning party in Egypt. Donald Malcolm Reid, 'Cairo University and the Orientalists', *International Journal of Middle East Studies*, 19 (1987), 51–76, usefully views Khalaf Allah in the light of the broader social context of the time.

12 Akhtar, op. cit., p. 69.

13 Ibid., pp. 70–1.

14 Ibid., p. 74.

15 For a brief but well-expressed appreciation, see W.A. Bijlefeld, 'In memoriam: Dr Fazlur Rahman', *Muslim World*, 79 (1989), 80–1.

16 Rahman, op. cit., p. 48, deals with moral ideals versus the legal plane on the issue of polygamy as an example of this.

17 Fazlur Rahman, *Islam*, 2nd edition, Chicago, IL, University of Chicago Press, 1979, pp. 38–9.

18 See Fazlur Rahman, *Islam and Modernity: Transformation of an Intellectual Tradition*, Chicago, IL, University of Chicago Press, 1982, Ch. 1.

19 A lucid introduction to his work may be found in Issa J. Boullata, *Trends and*

Issues in Contemporary Arab Thought, Albany, NY, State University of New York Press, 1990, pp. 79–85.

20 Mohammed Arkoun, 'The Death Penalty and Torture in Islamic Thought', *Concilium*, 120 (1979), 78.

21 See Boullata, op. cit., pp. 80–1.

22 Fatima Mernissi, *Beyond the Veil. Male–Female Dynamics in Modern Muslim Society*, revised edition, Bloomington, IN, Indiana University Press, 1987, p. 9.

7 FEMINISM'S 'NEW ISLAM'

1 For the reaction of men to these pressures see Yvonne Y. Haddad, *Contemporary Islam and the Challenge of History*, Albany, NY, State University of New York Press, 1982, pp. 54–70; our focus here is more on women's discussions than on male polemic-apologetic.

2 See the reflections of Susan E. Marshall, 'Paradoxes of Change: Culture Crisis, Islamic Revival, and the Reactivation of Patriarchy', *Journal of Asian and African Studies*, 19 (1984), 1–17.

3 Fatima Mernissi, *Beyond the Veil. Male–Female Dynamics in Modern Muslim Society*, revised edition, Bloomington, IN, Indiana University Press, 1987, pp. xxii–xxix. The status of older women may comprise a third category in between these two, but it is far less problematic a group for the jurists in the way in which they have understood the legal requirements.

4 Lois Beck, 'The Religious Lives of Muslim Women', in Jane I. Smith, ed., *Women in Contemporary Muslim Societies*, Lewisburg, PA, Bucknell University Press, 1980, pp. 27–60. See also Fatima Mernissi, 'Women, Saints, and Sanctuaries', *Signs: Journal of Women in Culture and Society*, 3 (1977), 101–12; Robert A. Fernea and Elizabeth W. Fernea, 'Variation in Religious Observance among Islamic Women', in Nikki R. Keddie, ed., *Scholars, Saints, and Sufis. Muslim Religious Institutions in the Middle East since 1500*, Berkeley, CA, University of California Press, 1972, pp. 385–401; among the many anthropological studies which examine the roles women play in Muslim societies, see the exemplary book of Janice Boddy, *Wombs and Alien Spirits: Women, Men and the Zar Cult in Northern Sudan*, Madison, WI, University of Wisconsin Press, 1989.

5 Mernissi, *Beyond the Veil*, op. cit., p. 82.

6 Alifa Rifaat, *Distant View of a Minaret and Other Stories* (trans. Denys Johnston-Davies), London, Heinemann, 1985.

7 Mernissi, *Beyond the Veil*, op. cit., p. xv.

8 Maulana Muhammad Ali, *The Religion of Islam: A Comprehensive Discussion of the Sources, Principles and Practices of Islam*, Columbus, OH, Ahmadiyya Anjuman Isha'at Islam, 1990 (revised 6th edition; first published 1936). While this quote comes from an Ahmadi writer (and thus from a 'suspect' source in many parts of the Islamic world), most Muslims would have no difficulty in agreeing with the sentiment expressed in it at this point; the modernist stance of Muhammad Ali's writing indicates that the idea of the natural inclinations of men and women as dictating their roles in society is far more widespread than just in Radical Islamist circles (in which it is the standard motif of discussions). Whether it is possible to deny these 'natural' differences (or to what extent one may do so) continues to plague North American feminist thought; see Carol Tavris, *The*

Mismeasure of Woman, New York, Simon and Schuster, 1992, who argues, for example, that studies show that men placed in the role of nurturer do just as well as women, and that women are as capable as men of acts of extreme violence.

9 Hajji Shaykh Yusuf (trans. Charles R. Pittman), 'In Defense of the Veil', *The Muslim World*, 33 (1943), 209, reprinted in Benjamin Rivlin and Joseph S. Szyliowicz, eds, *The Contemporary Middle East*, New York, Random House, 1965, p. 358.

10 An idea echoed in certain North American feminist analyses of their own society: e.g. the feminist classic, Susan Brownmiller, *Against Our Will: Men, Women and Rape*, New York, Simon and Schuster, 1975.

11 See the discussion of this point in Deniz A. Kandiyoti, 'Emancipated but Unliberated? Reflections on the Turkish Case', *Feminist Studies*, 13 (1987), 317–38. Some people of course may argue that a 'secure sense of gender identity' is not necessarily a welcome end.

12 See the statement by Saddeka Arebi, 'Gender Anthropology in the Middle East: The Politics of Muslim Women's Misrepresentation', *American Journal of Islamic Social Sciences*, 8 (1991), 99–108.

13 Jane I. Smith, 'The Experience of Muslim Women', in Yvonne Y. Haddad, Byron Haines and Ellison Findly, eds, *The Islamic Impact*, Syracuse, NY, Syracuse University Press, 1984, p. 112, n. 21, citing Mawdudi.

14 Among her many writings, see Riffat Hassan, 'An Islamic Perspective', in Jeanne Becher, ed., *Women, Religion and Sexuality: Studies on the Impact of Religious Teachings on Women*, Philadelphia, PA, Trinity Press, 1991, pp. 93–128; Hassan, 'On Human Rights and the Qur'anic Perspective', *Journal of Ecumenical Studies*, 19 (1982), 51–65; Hassan, 'Equal before Allah? Woman–Man Equality in the Islamic Tradition', *Harvard Divinity Bulletin*, 17 (1987), 2–4.

15 Shaista Aziz Alam, 'Purdah and the Qur'an', *Hamdard Islamicus*, 13 (1990), 82.

16 See the discussion in Jane I. Smith, 'Women in Islam: Equity, Equality, and the Search for the Natural Order', *Journal of the American Academy of Religion*, 47 (1979), 517–37

17 See Leila Ahmed, 'Women and the Advent of Islam', *Signs: Journal of Women in Culture and Society*, 11 (1986), 665–91, and her book, *Women and Gender in Islam: Historical Roots of a Modern Debate*, New Haven, CT, Yale University Press, 1992.

18 Nawal al-Sa'dawi, *Qadiyat al-Mar'a al-Misriyya al-Siyasiyya wa'l-Jinsiyya*, Cairo, 1977, trans. and quoted in Valerie J. Hoffman-Ladd, 'Polemics on the Modesty and Segregation of Women in Contemporary Egypt', *International Journal of Middle East Studies*, 19 (1987), 35.

19 See the comments in Yvonne Y. Haddad, 'Islam, Women and Revolution in Twentieth-Century Arab Thought', *The Muslim World*, 74 (1984), 137–60.

8 THE PRACTICE OF ISLAM

1 See the observations in Charles J. Adams, 'Islamic Resurgence: Religion and Politics in the Muslim World', in Nigel Biggar, Jamie S. Scott and William Schweiker, eds, *Cities of Gods. Faith, Politics and Pluralism in Judaism, Christianity and Islam*, New York, Greenwood Press, 1986, pp. 167–91, esp. p. 169.

2 See Malise Ruthven, *A Satanic Affair. Salman Rushdie and the Rage of Islam*, London, Chatto and Windus, 1990, pp.132–3 for further reflections along this line.

3 Note, for example, the study by M. Ali Kettani, *Muslim Minorities in the World Today*, London, Mansell, 1986, and the focus of interest revealed in the *Journal: Institute of Muslim Minority Affairs*.

4 Michael M.J. Fischer and Mehdi Abedi, *Debating Muslims: Cultural Dialogues in Postmodernity and Tradition*, Madison, WI, University of Wisconsin Press, 1990, p. 303. This book is a valuable treatment from an anthropological perspective of diaspora Muslim adjustment (as well as covering many other topics of interest).

5 Sayyid Abul A'la Mawdudi, *Let Us be Muslims* (ed. Khurram Murad), Leicester, The Islamic Foundation, 1985, p. 71 (first published in Urdu in 1940; also translated under the title *The Fundamentals of Islam*).

6 Rolf Reichert, 'Muslims in the Guyanas: A Socio-economic Overview', *Journal: Institute of Muslim Minority Affairs*, 3 (1981), 123; also cited in Kettani, op. cit., pp. 203–5. The problem is said by Reichert (pp. 123–4) to stem from the 'ignorance of the *shari'a*' on the part of the Javanese, but that hardly seems sufficient as an explanation of the issue.

7 S.D. Goitein, 'The Origin and Nature of the Muslim Friday Worship', in his *Studies in Islamic History and Institutions*, Leiden, E.J. Brill, 1966, p. 125.

8 Ruthven, op. cit., p. 72, also p. 158.

9 For some reflections on this issue, see Earle H. Waugh, 'The Imam in the New World. Models and Modifications', in Frank E. Reynolds and Theodore M. Ludwig, eds, *Transitions and Transformations in the History of Religions. Essays in Honor of Joseph M. Kitagawa*, Leiden, E.J. Brill, 1980, pp. 124–49.

10 This statement is found in the pamphlet, 'Concepts of Worship in Islam', distributed by the World Assembly of Muslim Youth from Riyadh, Saudi Arabia.

11 'The True Religious Value of Daily Prayers', *Hong Kong Muslim Herald*, 14 (Rabi-Thani 1412 AH: October 1991), p. 2–2 [sic].

12 Habib Bourguiba, 'For Ramadan Reform', in Benjamin Rivlin and Joseph S. Szyliowicz, eds, *The Contemporary Middle East: Tradition and Innovation*, New York, Random House, 1965, pp. 169–73 (reprinted from an address by President Bourguiba on 6 February 1961, according to this source, translated and published by the Tunisian Secretariat of State for Information); Francis Hours, 'A propos du jeûne du mois de Ramadan en Tunisie', *Orient*, 13 (1960), 43–52; S.D. Goitein, 'Ramadan, the Muslim Month of Fasting', in his *Studies*, op. cit., pp. 106–8.

13 Hava Lazarus-Yafeh, 'Contemporary Religious Thought among the 'Ulama of al-Azhar', in her *Some Religious Aspects of Islam. A Collection of Articles*, Leiden, E.J. Brill, 1981, p. 98.

14 J. Jomier and J. Corbon, 'Le Ramadan, au Caire, en 1956', *Mélanges d'institut dominicain d'études orientales du Caire*, 3 (1956), 1–74, esp. pp. 46–8.

15 Kamil al-Shinnawi, 'Against Ramadan Reform', reprinted in Rivlin and Szyliowicz, op. cit., pp. 174–8.

16 Albert Hourani, *Arabic Thought in the Liberal Age 1798–1939*, 2nd edition, Cambridge, Cambridge University Press, 1983, p. 350.

17 See Cyril Glassé, *The Concise Encyclopedia of Islam*, New York, HarperCollins, 1989, pp. 81–4, s.v. 'Calendar'; see also the discussion in Jomier and Corbon, op. cit., pp. 8–12.

18 See Lazarus-Yafeh, op. cit., p. 96.
19 See M.A. Mannan, *Islamic Economics: Theory and Practice*, new and revised edition, London, Hodder and Stoughton, 1986, esp. Ch. 13, 'Some Aspects of Public Finance in Islam'. Mannan grapples with some of the difficulties in the modern implementation of *zakat* as a tax system, for example regarding the impact of inflation.
20 See the discussion in Ann Elizabeth Mayer, 'Islamization and Taxation in Pakistan', in Anita M. Weiss, ed., *Islamic Reassertion in Pakistan. The Application of Islamic Laws in a Modern State*, Syracuse, NY, Syracuse University Press, 1986, pp. 59–77, which also points out the difficulties involved in the differences between Sunni and Shi'i taxation systems and the implications of the government imposition of the Sunni version.
21 Lazarus-Yafeh, op. cit., pp. 101–2.
22 See Kenneth Cragg, *The Dome and the Rock. Jerusalem Studies in Islam*, London, SPCK, 1964, p. 51.
23 Ibid., p. 52, an argument attributed to Mahmud Shaltut.
24 'The Way of Zakat', *Asia Week*, 13 September 1991, p. 63.
25 For an overview, see J. Jomier, 'Le pèlerinage musulman vu du Caire vers 1960', *Mélanges d'institut dominicain d'études orientales du Caire*, 9 (1967), 1–72, and for details of the itinerary of the *hajj* see pp. 12–14.
26 Hava Lazarus-Yafeh, 'Modern Muslim Attitudes towards the Ka'ba and the Hadjdj: The Rise of Neo-fundamentalism in Contemporary Islam', in her *Some Religious Aspects of Islam*, op. cit., pp. 106–29.
27 Quoted in ibid., p. 111.
28 See J. Michot, 'La signification du pèlerinage (Hajj) dans trois brochures populaires égyptiennes', *Mélanges d'institut dominicain d'études orientales du Caire*, 18 (1988), 211–42.
29 See Richard Antoun's analysis of 'Ali Shari'ati's book *Hajj* in his *Muslim Preacher in the Modern World: A Jordanian Case Study in Comparative Perspective*, Princeton, NJ, Princeton University Press, 1989, pp. 176–82. Also see Fischer and Abedi, op. cit., Ch. 3.
30 These figures come from Fouad al-Farsy, *Modernity and Tradition. The Saudi Equation*, London, Kegan Paul International, 1990, pp. 28–33, derived from information provided by the Deputy Ministry of the Interior for Passport and Civil Status. This book was distributed in 1991 by the Ministry of Information, Kingdom of Saudi Arabia; it also provides a breakdown by country for pilgrimage participation in 1987, giving, according to the author, 'some indication of the religious devotion of Muslims of the different countries'.
31 *Asia Week*, 5 July 1991, p. 24.
32 'Hajj and the *Ummah*'s Modern International Relations', in Kalim Siddiqui, ed., *Issues in the Islamic Movement 1983–84*, London, Open Press, 1985, pp. 98–9.
33 David Long, *The Hajj Today. A Survey of the Contemporary Makkan Pilgrimage*, Albany, NY, State University of New York Press, 1979, p. 127; this work is an excellent presentation of the many issues related to the pilgrimage raised in the modern context.
34 Antoun, op. cit., p. 168. This mode of analysis of the *hajj* is also found in Juan Eduardo Campo, 'The Mecca Pilgrimage in the Formation of Islam in Modern Egypt', in Jamie Scott and Paul Simpson-Housley, eds, *Sacred Places and Profane Spaces: Essays in the Geographics of Judaism, Christianity and Islam*, Westport, CT, Greenwood Press, 1991, pp. 145–61; Campo's emphasis falls on

the impact of *hajj* participation within three levels of religious discourse: governmental, oppositional and popular.

35 Lazarus-Yafeh, 'Contemporary Religious Thought', op. cit., p. 96. See Glassé, op. cit., p. 444, for a map of the *mawaqit* and pp. 180–2 for his article on the *ihram*.

36 See Richard C. Martin, 'Pilgrimage; Muslim Pilgrimage', *Encyclopedia of Religion*, New York, Macmillan, 1987, vol. 11, p. 345. Other specific legal aspects which have been modified in most understandings of the *hajj* ritual are detailed in Jomier, op. cit., pp. 68–71, most of which reflect the impact of the large number of people involved and the precise scheduling of events.

37 On the overall economic impact of the *hajj* see the articles in *The Middle East* for August 1987 (pp. 25–6), and August 1988 (p. 31); also see Fischer and Abedi, op. cit., pp. 168–70; Long, op. cit., pp. 95–104.

38 Adams, op. cit., p. 169.

39 Fischer and Abedi, op. cit., p. 153.

CONCLUSIONS: CONTEMPORARY MUSLIM RELIGIOSITY

1 Richard T. Antoun, *Muslim Preacher in the Modern World: A Jordanian Case Study in Comparative Perspective*, Princeton, NJ, Princeton University Press, 1989, p. 248.

2 Reinhold Loeffler, *Islam in Practice. Religious Beliefs in a Persian Village*, Albany, NY, State University of New York Press, 1988, p. 246.

3 Morroe Berger, *Islam in Egypt Today. Social and Political Aspects of Popular Religion*, Cambridge, Cambridge University Press, 1970, p. 83 (see pp. 81–4 on the *mawlid*s in general); see also J.W. McPherson, *The Moulids of Egypt (Egyptian Saint-Days)*, Cairo, N.M. Press, 1941, who lists 126 *mawlid*s among both Muslims and Christians.

4 The way in which this aspect functions in Moroccan society – the monarchy is legitimated through its association with Muhammad – is the emphasis of M.E. Combs-Schilling, *Sacred Performances: Islam, Sexuality, and Sacrifice*, New York, Columbia University Press, 1989, esp. pp.160–74 on the *mawlid*.

5 See, for example, the poem by al-Barzanji (d. 1766), an extract of which (on the birth of Muhammad) is quoted in Andrew Rippin and Jan Knappert, eds, *Textual Sources for the Study of Islam*, Manchester, Manchester University Press, 1986 (reprinted Chicago, IL, University of Chicago Press, 1990), Section 3.2.1.

6 Earle H. Waugh, *The Munshidin of Egypt. Their World and Their Song*, Columbia, SC, University of South Carolina Press, 1989, p. 189, quoted and translated from a book entitled *Al-Qamus al-Jadid fi' l-Qasa' id wa' l-Anashid*, published in Cairo, which Waugh describes as a collection of panegyric poems used by professional religious singers in contemporary Egypt.

7 Ibid., p. 100.

8 An excellent summary of the position of Sufism in the eighteenth, nineteenth and twentieth centuries, with relevant bibliography, is found in Chapter 4 of Julian Baldick, *Mystical Islam. An Introduction to Sufism*, London, I.B. Taurus, 1989.

Further reading

For a basic introduction to the scholarly study of Islam, see Volume 1 of this book, Andrew Rippin, *Muslims: Their Religious Beliefs and Practices. Volume 1: The Formative Period*, London, Routledge, 1990.

A recent reference work useful for many points of fact is Cyril Glassé, *The Concise Encyclopedia of Islam*, New York, HarperCollins, 1989; paperback edition San Francisco, Harper, 1991. Some of the entries in this book need to be handled with care, however, due to their universalistic mystical interpretations.

Francis Robinson, *Atlas of the Islamic World since 1500*, New York, Facts on File, 1982, is a nicely illustrated and useful reference which provides a basic historical orientation to the subject.

Some journals are of special importance in the study of modern Islam. Articles in *The Muslim World* frequently provide good coverage of basic issues, often providing the best introductory treatments. *International Journal of Middle Eastern Studies* tends towards social-scientific approaches on detailed issues. Other prominent journals worth surveying include *Middle East Journal* (emphasis on politics), *Middle Eastern Studies*, *American Journal of Islamic Social Sciences*, *Journal: Institute of Muslim Minority Affairs* and *Die Welt des Islam* (articles are frequently in English).

The following reading list comprises some of the more significant and informative works for the study of contemporary Islamic religious thought. Reference should be made to the notes of this volume for readings on specific issues.

Adams, Charles C., *Islam and Modernism in Egypt. A Study of the Modern Reform Movement Inaugurated by Muhammad 'Abduh*, London, Oxford University Press, 1933.

Ahmad, Aziz, *Islamic Modernism in India and Pakistan 1857–1964*, London, Oxford University Press, 1967.

—— and G.E. von Grunebaum, *Muslim Self-Statement in India and Pakistan 1857–1968*, Wiesbaden, Otto Harrassowitz, 1970. [Bio-bibliographical introduction; translated sources.]

Arkoun, Mohammed, *Lectures du Coran*, Paris, Editions G.-P. Maisonneuve et Larose, 1982.

Baljon, J.M.S., *Modern Muslim Koran Interpretation (1880-1960)*, Leiden, E.J. Brill, 1961.

Berque, Jacques, *The Arabs: Their History and Future* (trans. Jean Stewart), London, Faber and Faber, 1964.

Binder, Leonard, *Islamic Liberalism: A Critique of Development Ideologies*, Chicago, IL, University of Chicago Press, 1988.

Boullata, Issa J., *Trends and Issues in Contemporary Arab Thought*, Albany, NY, State University of New York Press, 1990.

Carré, Olivier, *Mystique et politique. Lecture révolutionnaire du Coran par Sayyid Qutb, frère musulman radical*, Paris, Les Éditions Du Cerf/Presses de la Fondation Nationale Des Sciences Politiques, 1984.

Cragg, Kenneth, *Counsels in Contemporary Islam*, Edinburgh, Edinburgh University Press, 1965.

——, *The Pen and the Faith. Eight Modern Muslim Writers and the Qur'an*, London, George Allen and Unwin, 1985.

Ede, David, Leonard Librande, Donald P. Little, Andrew Rippin and Richard Timms, *Guide to Islam*, Boston, MA, G.K. Hall, 1983. [A good bibliographical tool.]

Esposito, John L., ed., *Voices of Resurgent Islam*, New York, Oxford University Press, 1983.

——, *Islam and Politics*, Syracuse, NY, Syracuse University Press, 1984.

—— and John J. Donohue, eds, *Islam in Transition: Muslim Perspectives*, New York, Oxford University Press, 1982.

Fischer, Michael M.J. and Mehdi Abedi, *Debating Muslims. Cultural Dialogues in Postmodernity and Tradition*, Madison, WI, University of Wisconsin Press, 1990.

Geertz, Clifford, *Islam Observed. Religious Developments in Morocco and Indonesia*, New Haven, CT, Yale University Press, 1968.

Gibb, Hamilton A.R., *Modern Trends in Islam*, Chicago, IL, University of Chicago Press, 1947.

Gilsenan, Michael, *Recognizing Islam: Religion, and Society in the Modern Middle East*, London, Croom Helm, 1982.

Grunebaum, Gustave E. von, *Modern Islam. The Search for Cultural Identity*, Berkeley, CA, University of California Press, 1962.

Haddad, Yvonne Yazbeck, *Contemporary Islam and the Challenge of History*, Albany, NY, State University of New York Press, 1982.

——, ed., *The Muslims of America*, New York, Oxford University Press, 1991.

——, Byron Haines and Ellison Findly, eds, *The Islamic Impact*, Syracuse, NY, Syracuse University Press, 1984.

—— and Adair T. Lummis, *Islamic Values in the United States. A Comparative Study*, New York, Oxford University Press, 1987.

——, John Obert Voll and John L. Esposito, *The Contemporary Islamic Revival: A Critical Survey and Bibliography*, New York, Greenwood Press, 1991.

Hourani, Albert, *Arabic Thought in the Liberal Age, 1798–1939*, London, Oxford University Press, 2nd edition, 1983.

Jansen, J.J.G., *The Interpretation of the Koran in Modern Egypt*, Leiden, E.J. Brill, 1974.

Juynboll, G.H.A., *The Authenticity of the Tradition Literature. Discussions in Modern Egypt*, Leiden, E.J. Brill, 1969.

Kerr, Malcolm H., *Islamic Reform. The Political and Legal Theories of Muhammad 'Abduh and Rashid Rida*, Berkeley, CA, University of California Press, 1966.

Lawrence, Bruce B., *Defenders of God: The Fundamentalist Revolt against the Modern Age*, San Francisco, CA, Harper and Row, 1989.

McDonough, Sheila, *The Authority of the Past. A Study of Three Muslim Modernists*, Chambersburg, PA, American Academy of Religion, 1970.

Mortimer, Edward, *Faith and Power. The Politics of Islam*, New York, Random House, 1982.

Munson, Henry, Jr, *Islam and Revolution in the Middle East*, New Haven, CT, Yale University Press, 1988.

Nielson, Jorgen, *Muslims in Western Europe*, Edinburgh, Edinburgh University Press, 1992.

Rahman, Fazlur, *Major Themes of the Qur'an*, Minneapolis, MN, Bibliotheca Islamica, 1980.

——— *Islam and Modernity. Transformation of an Intellectual Tradition*, Chicago, IL, University of Chicago Press, 1982.

Sabanegh, E.S., *Muhammad b. Abdallah, 'Le prophète'. Portraits contemporains Egypte 1930–1950*, Paris, Librairie J. Vrin, n.d.

Sivan, Emmanuel, *Radical Islam: Medieval Theology and Modern Politics*, New Haven, CT, Yale University Press, 1985.

Smith, Wilfred Cantwell, *Islam in Modern History*, Princeton, NJ, Princeton University Press, 1957.

Index